GODDESS RUNES

Other Books by
P. M. H. Atwater

BEYOND THE LIGHT
COMING BACK TO LIFE
FUTURE MEMORY

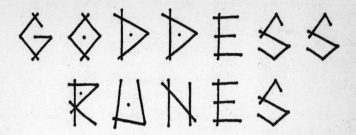

GODDESS RUNES

A Comprehensive Guide to Casting and Divination with one of the Oldest Known Rune Sets

P.M.H. ATWATER

AVON BOOKS ◆ NEW YORK

GODDESS RUNES is an original publication of Avon Books. This version of the work has never before appeared in book form.

AVON BOOKS
A division of
The Hearst Corporation
1350 Avenue of the Americas
New York, New York 10019

Library of Congress Cataloging in Publication Data:

Atwater, P. M. H.
  Goddess Runes / P.M.H. Atwater.
    p.   cm.
  Includes bibliographical references and index.
  1. Runes—Miscellanea. 2. Divination. 3. Goddess religion. I. Title.
BF1891.R85A62   1996   95-50286
133.3'3—dc20   CIP

First Avon Books Trade Printing: July 1996

AVON TRADEMARK REG. U.S. PAT. OFF. AND IN OTHER COUNTRIES, MARCA REGISTRADA, HECHO EN U.S.A.

Printed in the U.S.A.

OPM   10 9 8 7 6 5 4 3 2 1

This book is dedicated to the millions of people, male and female, who are ready to reclaim the truth of their own inner wisdom.

Goddess Runes and The Way of A Cast lead beyond what is known of myths and legends to the feminine principle of balance and wholeness, and to the beginnings of all beginnings at the primordial dream-pool of our first memories as human beings.

Prepare yourself . . . for each turn of the page will bring you steadily closer to the earth magic of "freezing" or stopping time (so you can examine one moment and what it might mean—how divination works), and to the soul magic of self-empowerment (so you can grow in confidence of your own worth—how maturity works).

Our deeper depths is the subject, the sacredness of play our focus. Welcome to a magical, mystical journey through the wonderful world of runes.

The following people made this book possible. To each I extend my deepest gratitude:

Dana Corby, who originally introduced me to the "Runes of Njord," then disappeared, only to turn up fifteen years later with a friendly letter of hello, admitting that it was she who had coined their title, for the runes had been but a nameless set.

Tricia Horne, who, from our first meeting in the late seventies, urged me to write a book about the yin runes I used and the feminine principle of casting.

Dennis Swartz, who refused to give me a moment's peace until I not only self-published but revised my original version of *The Magical Language of Runes* for a softcover edition through Bear & Company.

Barbara Hand Clow, the co-publisher at Bear & Company, who renamed my book *Goddess Runes* and urged me to find a larger press so the book could have a more diverse audience.

David Morgan, one of my literary agents, who transcended his professional status to become a thoughtful shepherd of the book's evolution from a self-published experiment, through a brief stint as a Bear book, to its reemergence with Avon Books.

Charlotte Abbott, my editor at Avon Books, who fell in love with *Goddess Runes* and nursed it with great care and devotion through the editing and rewriting processes.

Contents

GODDESS RUNES

Introduction

At a "Welcome to Boise, Idaho" party arranged to honor a troupe who had just moved into town from California, one woman (who I learned fifteen years later was named Dana Corby) said she practiced rune casting and, with our permission, would demonstrate what runes were and how they worked. No one at the party knew anything about runes, so we readily agreed to what seemed like a new form of entertainment.

The woman sat upon the floor and produced from a velvet pouch a handful of small, soft-black pebbles, each graven with a strange, sharp-angled glyph. She invited several people to ask questions of the stones, and said she would seek for answers by casting them. I remember most clearly the awe I felt as stones flew from her hands with each cast. In falling, they formed the most fascinating patterns—patterns that sprang to life for me in multiple textures of image, sound, smell—as if they possessed the vitality of pulse and breath. I was spellbound by their aliveness.

The woman's voice rambled past my awareness as I concentrated privately on each cast, interpreting for myself their meanings, correcting what seemed to be her mistakes, and adding additional insights. When she finished with the demonstration, she turned abruptly in my direction and stated out loud, "You can read these runes better than I." Before I knew what was happening or why, I heard myself reply, "You're correct. I can."

While other people expressed excitement about the strange runes, I quietly pondered what had just occurred. I had never seen runes before and knew nothing consciously of their history or usage. Yet, suddenly, I knew them as well as if I had created them. This puzzled me.

Later, after almost everyone else had left, I was finally able to speak with the woman. When I asked why she had said what she did, her answer only puzzled me more: "I knew you knew." There was a mysterious smile on her lips when she said that, and I found myself requesting a pouch of stones like hers before I had a chance to think. "For fifteen dollars I'll make you a set," she said, and then went on to explain what kind of stones worked best and how each would be selected. "You're getting a bargain, you know, for I meditate on each pebble to make certain that both glyph and stone fit each other perfectly. The pouch is all hand-sewn." I accepted.

Several weeks went by until, on the night of the full moon, during a prayer-and-meditation gathering, she appeared and presented me with the finished pouch of pebbles. I paid her, but felt a strong inner sense not to open the pouch, that it must first be blessed and dedicated as part of the evening's spiritual service.

Using the enhanced energies I felt at the service, I enclosed the pouch within my cupped hands and, in my mind's eye, envisioned beams and splashes of radiant light and pure love filling and cleansing the new bundle. In prayer, I asked for divine guidance to know how and when to cast the runes, and then I dedicated them to God's Holy Will. The pouch grew hot and tingled as if an electric current had passed through it. Afterward, I gently placed the rune pouch in my purse and spoke no more of it.

A week later I left Boise, Idaho, literally closing the door on a lifetime and leaving behind everything and everyone I had ever known. This was in August of 1978.

A year and a half before, I had physically died three times, revived after each episode, only to suffer three major relapses that same year. I was now newly healed. During those episodes when death had come to call, I had undergone the phenomenon known as the near-death experience; that is to say, I had crossed over to The Other Side. Each experience had been different, yet each one had somehow led into the next as if they were progressive. This had affected me so radically that life on earth lost relevance. Thus, it had become necessary for me to relearn the basics: from having to crawl and stand to telling the difference between left and right, from seeing and hearing properly to rebuilding my belief systems. In the course of doing this, I discovered myself to be different from before. Somehow I had expanded both in my capacity for analysis and inquiry and in my ability to detect and respond to subtle energies and impressions.

In this new state, I sold a house I had recently purchased; gave away, sold, or stored everything I owned; and quit an excellent job the very day a major promotion and raise were offered. What seemed necessary for survival I stuffed into my little Ford Pinto. The next day I embarked on a spiritual odyssey that led first to the Shanti Nilaya Center of Elisabeth Kübler-Ross, at that time located near Escondido, California, where I shared with others the discovery we were all making—that there is life after death. From there I zigzagged across the entire continent, leaving behind the Pacific's silver sunsets to find to my delight that sunrises over the Atlantic are indeed drenched with gold.

It was during this odyssey, near the "knife's edge" of the Grand Canyon's deepest drop, that I opened the rune pouch for the first time and spilled across my lap the strange stones, all sixteen of them, complete with brief instructions for their use in casting. I felt like a child again, holding my new toys. From that moment on I played with them daily, experimenting, studying every possible variation and nuance of question and throw. Sometimes I would involve others in my play, even groups of others, as I probed further, wondering if I could manipulate answers with my mind and thereby control or direct a cast.

There wasn't anything I didn't try. No question or throw was too absurd or too complex or too impossible. I even tallied the accuracy or inaccuracy of each result on a written scorecard.

During this playtime, I noticed a few peculiarities about using casting runes. When I read for others, patterns of the cast would change according to how each individual *felt* about the question he or she asked of the runes. *Unexpressed motives behind the questions* would alter or change the outcome. Runic answers would invariably address what was *most important for the querist to know,* rather than the exact question asked. I also found that runes would answer my own questions the same way they did for everyone else *if I was honest enough to be objective and detached.*

I came to realize that I could not control or direct rune casts in any manner, even on my own behalf. The runestones always remained independent, obeying faithfully whatever laws governed their movement and whatever source guided their revelations. They were not toys and I did not "own" them. I came to regard them as friends, and in our friendship, we became equal partners on the same team.

With the passing of years, our teamwork arrangement evolved. The pouch transformed into a "Medicine Bag" in the sense that I eventually filled it with all manner of symbolic reminders of sacredness and unity. Native American teachings of "The Medicine Path," a lifestyle anyone can adopt that is dedicated to the responsible service of healing and helping others, came naturally to me, so I integrated my rune friends and The Way of A Cast into that worldview.

Later, while researching runic legends and stories, I took special interest in the tales of Odin (in Germanic lore) and how he "died unto himself" (had a near-death experience) before the secrets of the runes were revealed to him. Facing one's own death, whether symbolically or literally, seems to have been a prerequisite for a shaman, or "wise one," to understand the deeper meaning of rune signs in the Old European cultures that originally developed runes. Each tribal grouping had its own tradition for testing initiates through a simulation of death, so the individual could transcend his or her ego and become spiritually transformed. Rune use altered drastically, though, when alphabets were later adopted and tribal clans became more sophisticated. What was once an earned privilege for the purpose of accessing greater wisdoms evolved into a routine skill for the purpose of marking public inscriptions and recording the ownership of property. Secular designs and usages can be traced historically, but only fragments remain of the older, more sacred glyphs and the manner in which they were used.

The fact that the concepts of death, transformation, and rebirth were so entwined with ancient rune use affected me deeply, and I could not help but wonder about the timeliness of their entry into my life. It seemed no accident that runes came to me when they did, after my own journey through death's portal.

During my youth in Idaho, I spent my earliest years in a Norwegian household that honored traditions unique to the Sogne Fjord region of Norway. Although no one ever mentioned runes, the mind-set of a culture that once used them was nonetheless instilled in me. Having temporarily lost a sense of personal history after my near-death experiences, I regained not only my memories but the ability to tap into any form of memory—be it from a rock or from collective sources of human consciousness. I was able, quite literally, to retrain how I used my brain because of the unique way rune casting seems to unite left and right brain hemispheres—resulting in a healthy whole.

Goddess Runes is my way of saying ''Thank you'' to the runes and passing along the art form of casting to others. Truly, this is a book of love.

CHAPTER ONE

What History Tells Us

Once upon a time, actually about twenty thousand to twenty-three thousand years ago, our forebears, the Cro-Magnon people, were an intelligent lot, sleek of body and immensely creative. Having invented the needle, they wore tailored clothes complete with decorated tunics and leggings, parkas, collared shirts with cuffed sleeves, and boots and moccasins. They built most of their dwellings facing south to take advantage of solar heat, fashioned ingenious cobblestone floors that were sturdy and dry, preserved food year-round in cold caves, ate diets so healthy we moderns would be wise to emulate them, crafted clever tools (such as a sewing needle complete with hole for thread), separated living spaces for greater efficiency, and eventually took to the water in boats for better fishing.[1]

Their cave art enthralls anyone lucky enough to see it, especially the recently discovered paintings in caves near Combe d'Arc, about 260 miles south of Paris. These stunning rock galleries depict half-human/half-animal figures and extinct European cousins of African beasts, lending even more credibility to the theory that a land bridge must have connected the continents, and that the entire world's population might have indeed descended from one group of pioneers who started out from Africa.

Most archaeologists now credit our Cro-Magnon forebears

with bringing forth the first script like unto hieroglyphs that seemed to convey sacred and spiritual truths. In his landmark text *Allmutter,* German professor Herman Wirth painstakingly documented the emergence of runic symbols about twenty thousand years ago.[2] More recently, Lithuanian-born archaeologist Marija Gimbutas has produced a scholarly rendering of the goddess-worshipping, matriarchal, prehistoric societies that among other things created a written "alphabet of the metaphysical" that today we recognize as runes.[3]

In an interview, she explained that most scholars don't understand how important religion was in the prehistory of Europe, how religion was life and life was religion. She posits that the sacred scripts of rune signs were feeling-oriented and in wide use from at least 17000 B.C. As Gimbutas states in her masterpiece, *The Civilization of the Goddess: The World of Old Europe:*

> Although the Sumerians are generally thought to be the inventors of written language, a script in east-central Europe appeared some two thousand years earlier than any other that has yet been found. Unlike Sumerian script, the writing of the Old Europeans was not devised for economic, legal, or administrative purposes. It was developed, instead, from a long use of graphic symbolic signs found only within the context of an increasingly sophisticated worship of the Goddess. Inscriptions appear on religious items only, indicating that these signs were intended to be read as sacred hieroglyphs.[4]

To appreciate Gimbutas's claims and how work such as hers impacts on our understanding of runes, join me on a brief excursion through the history of language, alphabets, symbols, and signs. Modern scholars have made the distant past more accessible to us, and infinitely more exciting than what used to pose as "History 101" when we went to high school. Just by focusing in on linguistics, we encounter evidence that suggests . . . we all share common roots.

For example, John Philip Cohane, an Irish etymologist (one who studies historical linquistics), said in his challenging book, *The Key:* "On the basis of the evidence, it would seem that a high percentage of the people of the earth today are far more closely related than is generally assumed, and that they are bound together by at least one blood stream."[5] Alessandro Talamonti, an Italian archaeologist now living in Venezuela, elaborates further during an interview held several years ago: "A mother civilization was once basically uniform the world over. All people share the same language, the same religion, and practically the same customs."

Gerhard Herm, author of *The Celts,* hypothesizes an Ur-language, Ur-people, and Ur-homeland ("Ur" meaning "original") in an attempt to explain how Sanskrit, the ancient metaphysical language of India, could be so closely related to the early languages of Old Europe, especially that of Iceland. He posits that Ur-people came across a land bridge and spread across the Baltics, the former Soviet Union, Europe, and Asia, reshaping their language, customs, and culture as they went.[6]

"You have to respect the idea that all the languages were related 25,000 years ago," agrees Winfred P. Lehmann, a retired professor of linguistics and Germanic languages at the University of Texas at Austin. As he points out, "We can learn more about prehistory through language, possibly where civilization actually developed. Words give us a notion of what people were talking about, and thus something about their culture."[7]

Recognizable alphabet characters in specific languages began to emerge about six thousand years ago, interestingly enough at about the same time as a dazzling spectacle in the sky occurred. Astronomers label this phenomenon Supernova Vela X. George Michanowsky, an expert on ancient Mesopotamian astronomy, believes that this bright "star" became an organizing principle that drew people in given areas together in an attempt to share their awe, and that this one event greatly accelerated the evolution of human consciousness. He notes in his book, *The Once and Future Star,* that virtually all of the world's great myths

and religions emphasize this star, and that the star symbol is
found on more relics and in more ancient sites than any other
design (followed in popularity, I might add, by spirals and
chevrons).[8]

All the early alphabets were cleverly crafted to contain "en-
cyclopedias" of layered meaning. That's what makes them so
difficult to decipher. In *Before Columbus,* renowned historian
and linguist Cyrus Herzl Gordon explains that not only were
the early alphabet letters interchangeable for sounds, numbers,
and signs of the heavens, they were actually a code language
of unmistakable coherence.[9]

Many historians agree that this code language was tied to a
desire for Holy Revelation, since ... *every early language had
as its central core the need to communicate a relationship with
The Source of All Being.* Thus, the names of God revealed the
power of God through the forms God takes as the Logos—the
sound of The Holy Word.

If truth be known, these early alphabets merely continued an
older tradition ... never representative, the symbol signs were
considered to be *the thing itself,* both magical and sacred. To
this day, a primary rule in the practice of "magick" insists that
sacred images do not *refer,* they *are.*

Runic alphabet characters were eventually used for charms
and spells, curses and omens, as if each were a living deity of
great importance and possessed of the power to manifest.

"Because in magic a symbol *is* what it stands for, to write
down a wish or a curse in symbols automatically gives effect
to what is written. In the same way, runes were engraved on
swords to make them irresistible in battle, as in the case of a
sword named Marr—'may Marr spare nobody,' " says Richard
Cavendish, an expert on "magick." He notes that writing with
a pen did not reach northern Europe until Christian missionaries
brought the art with them; runic inscriptions were carved—
usually on wood, tombstones, jewels, standing stones, equipment, and tools of all kinds. He emphasized that

Writing is a mysterious and magical art. In many primitive
and ancient societies it was assumed that the gods must

have invented this marvelous method of capturing speech and turning it into visible form. In the ancient world the fact that most people could not write, or read what was written, and that those who could were usually priests, brought writing a reputation as a great hidden wisdom. And its use in inscriptions on the tombs of the dead gave it a close connection with the other world.[10]

The tumultuous years between 1500 B.C. and 15 B.C., when most of the world's great religions sprang into being (Taoism, Confucianism, Zoroastrianism, Jainism, Buddhism, Judaism, and, later, Christianity), comprise *the same time frame* in which "Futhark," the codified version of runes, is believed to have taken hold. Supposedly named "Futhark" because of the random combination of the first six letters in the alphabet's arrangement, the ancient "written-but-not-spoken" language developed into three major lineages:

Germanic—the first appearance was supposedly around 2000 B.C., although some historians staunchly insist that it did not exist until after A.D. 800.

Anglo-Saxon or English—most agree it lasted from the fifth century A.D. to the twelfth.

Northern or Viking/Scandinavian—the last to appear on the scene, probably in the eighth century and until the twelfth.

The name "rune" is a fairly recent term, and was originally thought to have evolved from the German word *raunen,* which means "to cut or carve." Yet an examination of older German dictionaries long since retired from general use reveals that *raunen* once meant "to whisper secrets" and "Rune" (always capitalized then) was the noun for "secret" (also written "Run" or "Runa").

I find it fascinating that the ancient Hawaiian term for "secret" was "Huna," similar to "Runa," and that both versions of the word shared the same understanding of "secret" as "the

RUNES TYPES

German Runes

English Runes

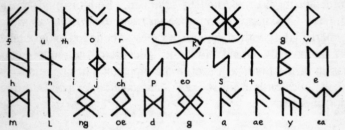

Scandinavian Runes

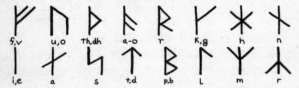

mystery of sacred truth.'' Equally curious to me is that ''Fohart'' in Sanskrit means ''the power to manifest and create words.'' Since ''Fohart'' and ''Futhark'' are nearly alike in pronunciation as well as spelling, I can't help but wonder if the name for the codified runic alphabets was really such a random call after all.

Secular use of the ''written-not-spoken'' language of runes evolved as the practical uses for written language and literacy became evident. Eventually, Futhark was broadly used to record family genealogies, battles, ownership, and announcements of all types. Stone and wood were the main media of choice, with

colors often added for emphasis. Later on, it became commonplace for rune writing to include fanciful works of art that incor-
porated animal images, snakelike creatures, and ringerikes—
intricate interweavings of vines and animal tails. (For further

RINGERIKES

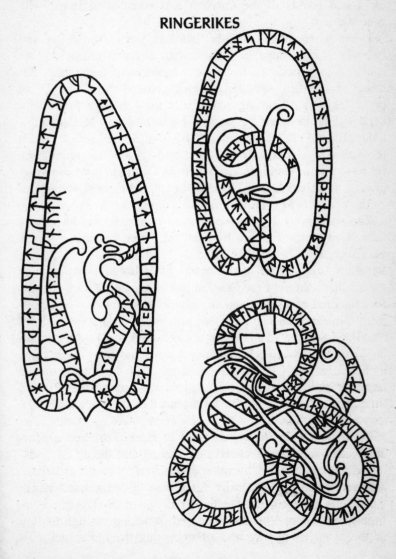

information about runic rituals and lore throughout this period in history, check Footnote 11 for a listing of references.)

There is no way one can speak of runes without at least mentioning ogam (or ogham). A "slash" script attributed to the Druid priests of the Celts, it was often interspersed with rune writing.

Ogam letters were typically "slashed," or carved above and below a stone's edge to form certain alphabet characters. As such, ogam is believed to be the antecedent of telegraphy. Because of its stark simplicity, ogam enabled the Celtic Druid priests to "sign" messages back and forth through finger-and-hand signals in much the same manner the deaf use "signing" today. Barry Fell, researcher and author of *America B.C.,* details the varied developments of ogam and how it has often been found to adorn American artifacts from Colorado to Maine (suggesting that Celts and/or Norsemen explored a good deal of our country *long before* the coming of Columbus).[12]

The older runic glyphs and how they are cast may have been influenced to some extent by the Lost Tribes of Israel.[13] Frank C. Tribbe describes tablets dated to 707 B.C. that tell of captive Israelites being taken to the towns of Halah and Habor, near the southern shore of the Caspian Sea in ancient Media, perhaps four hundred miles east and slightly north of the Assyrian capital of Nineveh. One group went northward on the east side of the Black Sea and within a century became known as the Scythians. Another group who went westward and then north came to be called the Cimmerians, a people who later took on the name "Celts." Tribbe quotes Josephus as saying that "in his time [A.D. 37 to 95] the ten northern tribes of Israel were then 'beyond the Black Sea.' "[14]

Scythians/Cimmerians were said to have possessed a ferocious passion. They practiced rune casting and the art of "raising sacral energies." "Sacral energies" refers to "Kundalini," a powerful force said to exist at the base of one's spine which, when fully charged or activated by intention or through ritual, supposedly "rises" up the spine and passes on through the top of the head, energizing and strengthening the individual as it

OGAM

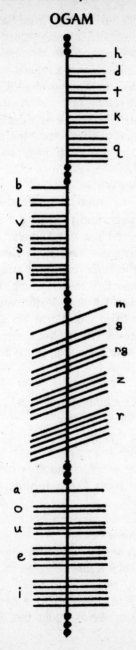

does. The term "Kundalini" comes from Sanskrit. The philosophy of these people included an acceptance of life after death, resurrection, reincarnation, and the absolute value of truth and honesty. Archaeological evidence suggests that ritualized human sacrifice was practiced in their societies, along with head-hunting, scalping, and ceremonial sex. As their numbers fanned out across Europe and Asia, they took their beliefs and practices with them, invading one goddess-worshipping, matrilineal community after another and establishing a pantheon of male warrior gods.

The legends of Odin/Wotan descend in part from this divergent mix of cultures in Europe. Accordingly, the Germanic god Odin (warrior, seer, poet, and God of the Hanged) is credited with having rediscovered the runic power of the older sacred scripts (while his Viking counterpart, Wotan, sometimes spelled "Woden," is given the same credit). Various versions of both stories are at least consistent in describing the circumstances of what we today would call a near-death experience—Odin hung transfixed by a spear from the World Tree, the ash Yggdrasil. Part of the legend appears here, the quote originating in *The Poetic Edda,* an Icelandic collection of myths translated by H.A. Bellows in 1923:

> *I know that I hung for nine whole nights*
> *Upon a windswept tree,*
> *Gashed by a spear and given to Odin,*
> *Myself given to myself,*
> *On the tree of which no man can tell*
> *From what roots it has sprung.*
>
> *No man served me with bread or drink;*
> *I peered down below,*
> *Took the runes up, shrieking took them,*
> *Then fell back again.*[15]

(As a brief aside, Wotan was also the name of a Mayan god. During the Chimu Empire, at about the time of the Spanish conquest of South America, each Peruvian temple boasted a statue of the god "Gutan," meaning "whirlwind." "Gutan" was originally written as "Wotan," and he was deemed Lord of Night and Darkness among Mayans, Aztecs, and Zapotecs, who all associated him with the art of divination—as in stories of the storm god Odin/Wotan. The ancient Mesoamerican myths of creation and the messiah figure of Quetzalcoatl are comparable to those of North America and Europe, except that legends of Quetzalcoatl are far older. Still, many of the songs and story-forms (a segment of oral history told as a story) of each group are the same or similar, suggesting perhaps another far-flung connection with rune lore[16] and indicating that the various types of rune signs and casting techniques may have been very broadly used and very old indeed.)

Regardless of what mythology you read from this later epoch of Celtic/Germanic/Viking/Anglo-Saxon history, there is reference after reference given to runes: runes everlasting, runes giving life, runes as magic signs, runes to invoke the gods and spirit keepers. Never does anyone simply say, "I know my alphabet letters." Rather, people tell how versed they are in "rune spells" (the writing or engraving of certain glyphs, perhaps singly or in combination, to meet a need or avoid a crisis). Even when runic letter script was well developed in secular alphabets, there was no divorcing it from a mystical heritage of vast proportions.

Runes always remained first and foremost a magical language of sacred truths and secret deeds. Secular embellishments appear almost as if incidental, an effrontery tolerated to accommodate a need for literacy.

Most of us, when we think of runes, conjure up images of Celtic warriors and their Druid priests or of Viking raiders and their attiba (wizards) and volva (female seers). Since both Celt and Norse societies held the religious aspect of life primary, rituals of every type defined their activities. Each culture worshipped a triune of powerful gods, plus hundreds of minor deities who varied in identity from place to place. These minor deities were representative of important aspects of the main gods and creation storyforms. Priests and practitioners committed everything to memory then, passing on their store of knowledge through a series of apprenticeships from generation to generation. Sacred law made no allowance for written records of any kind; violators were dealt with harshly.

Starkly different, Celts and Norse did share many common beliefs, such as veneration of great trees, cultivation of special herbs, disciplined personal regimens, the importance of wizardry, various types of sacrifice, and a whole world of wee helpers (e.g. fairies, gnomes, sprites, dwarves, trolls, leprechauns, and so forth). As both cultures modernized, so did their legends, until today we have *The Tales of King Arthur* from the Celtic tradition and *The Tales of Valhalla and the Valkyries* from the Norse tradition.

By the thirteenth century, Christian priests began a campaign to wipe out rune use, as they felt it was too closely aligned with pagan religious magic and therefore sinful. (The word "pagan," by the way, simply means "country dweller" in Latin; the word "magic" comes from Babylonian and Persian traditions of "magno," a reference to "receptivity"—"magnet," "magnetic," and "magi" are derived from the same root word.)

The Catholic Church, as a political maneuver in what came to be called the Inquisition, invented the term "witchcraft" so they could use unfounded accusations to gain absolute control over the masses. Hence, any form of nature worship, fertility rituals, birth control, herbal healing, shamanism, or sorcery was decreed the devil's work and outlawed. For a period of over three hundred years, tens of thousands of people were slaughtered, most of them women. Even in seventeenth-century Iceland, people were still being burned to death for the single "crime" of possessing runes.

As you can see from this brief historical excursion, runes and their usage have had a long and checkered past. What survives today are relics and myths, some describing far gentler times when runes were an integral part of uplifting the soul and gladdening the heart.

The legacy we have inherited from runes, however, is more diverse than I've mentioned.

Apart from script and alphabets, runes once existed as an art form called "runestone," which was very popular in the decoration of exquisite bowls, cups, and platters. The word "rune," interchangeable with the word for "cantos," signified the main divisions in a long song or poem. Speaking of runes evoked a kind of poetic cadence that brought to mind scenes of nature and a reverence for the pulse of life. Even though unspoken in regular speech, *runes were spoken in the symbolic speech* of lays—short "melodic" narratives. Not only were they spoken, they were sung. Runesingers and runechanters from many different cultural groups throughout millennia of time quite literally functioned as musical historians, preserving much of the early history we now study.

To speak of runes, truly, is to speak of poetry. To sing of runes is to join in chorus with the emotions life brings.

J.R.R. Tolkien probably understood this aspect of the power of runes when he created a type of ancestral writing in his timeless epics of Middle Earth entitled *The Hobbit, The Lord of the Rings,* and *The Silmarillion.*[17] Tolkien was a professional philologist (language expert), and spent his life studying the history and origins of the English language. Nobel Prize-winning author Rudyard Kipling has also delighted several generations of children with his version of rune writing in his *Just So Stories,*[18] which included a tale of how the first letter in the first alphabet ever came to be (naturally, that first letter was a runic glyph). Both men fashioned their fictional runes on archaeological findings.

A few centuries ago, runesingers, still hiding out from public view, prophesied that one day, through the hands of children and those with childlike minds, the magic of runes would be rediscovered and returned to the world.

Nine or ten years ago, while I was leafing through a catalog of Victorian antiques, I happened upon pictures of runes and rune pouches that were advertised as children's toys around the turn of this century. When I saw them I mused to myself about the old runesingers' prophecy and how true it is that children's toys and games have a strange and wonderful way of preserving spiritual wisdom. (The game of hopscotch, for example, is actually a symbolic representation of the Tree of Life in the Jewish Kabbala, a spiritual guide to understanding the universal mysteries; and it is played the same way its predecessor was studied. Also, jacks is an extension of rune casting, as a way to train hand/eye coordination and build a sense of confidence in one's abilities with the skill of the toss.)

Ralph Blum, intellectual-turned-intuitive, popularized the younger runes known as Futhark in his landmark offering that came in the early eighties, *The Book of Runes*.[19]

Across the eons of time in which runes can be traced, they have come to be typed in two major categories:

1. *The Elder Runes*—used primarily in free-form casting, *yin in energy,* representative of the feminine principle, closely associated with goddess religions and the veneration of home, family, and nature. Cast together as a single unit, they are free of restrictive formats or layouts. Illustrative, they highlight connections within a greater flow of possibility and the interactions of the moment. They always emphasize spiritual themes, inner guidance, and responsive patterning (never secularized).

2. *The Younger Runes*—used primarily as oracles, *yang in energy,* representative of the masculine principle, closely associated with the great hero-gods of mythology and the right use of power in personal behavior. Although they can be cast, they are usually taken from the pouch one at a time to emphasize a particular aspect or quality, according to specific guidelines governing usages and meaning. Instructive, they highlight individual decisions and opportunities. They always emphasize intuitive truth seeking (although secularized, they retain spiritual components).

The secret to using the elder runes, what this book is about, is *feeling* and *trust.*

(

Once you capture the *feeling* within each runic glyph, you reconnect with the true spirit of that imagery and the energy of the moment it seeks to illustrate. Because rune signs are textured with multiple layers of sacred and secular interpretations, you can empower yourself with the confidence it takes to trust the wisdom of your own inner guidance.

The yin runes of the goddess lay bare the flowing patterns of the heart.

CHAPTER TWO

Goddess Runes

Most of the symbol signs in the runic system I use appear in the listing Marija Gimbutas made of sacred scripts in her book *The Civilization of the Goddess: The World of Old Europe.* The dates she gave for the scripts ranged from seventeen thousand to fourteen thousand years ago. Professor Wirth dated them back even farther. There is ample evidence in cave art, with artifacts, and through myth and oral histories to support any dating in advance of 12000 B.C.

No question, elder runes are ancient, and the ones I present in this book are part of that antiquity.

Because I have been unable to document directly the full lineage of the set I keep, the statements I make in this book about them are based on a combination of historical research, my own knowledge of symbology, the "flood" of information concerning their past that has come to me since they entered my life, and the experience of having cast them thousands upon thousands of times for more people than I can count.

I was told they were called the "Runes of Njord" when I was first introduced to them at that "Welcome to Boise, Idaho" party back in 1978. I continued to use that name in *The Magical Language of Runes,*[20] the self-published book I wrote about them and The Way of A Cast that was later picked up by Bear & Company. It wasn't until fifteen years later that Dana

Corby, the woman who had originally demonstrated the runes to me, set the record straight. It was she who had named them. They had been nameless when passed on to her from her teacher. Where her teacher had obtained them she did not know.

When I wanted to revise *The Magical Language of Runes,* it was the co-publisher at Bear & Company, Barbara Hand Clow, who suggested that I call the new version *Goddess Runes* and that I should come out with an expanded edition. I took Clow's advice, but went one step further—I gave the runes themselves the name Clow gave my book, for they have long since earned that title by right of virtue and historical record: they truly are . . . Goddess Runes.

With that said, allow me to introduce you to them.

The Goddess Runes set consists of sixteen small, somewhat flat stones, two of them unmarked for the asking of questions and fourteen message carriers that "wear" a carved runic glyph upon them.

The pebbles in the set I have are river-worn and from a stream in Mexico. They are soft black in color and engraved on one side (although they just as easily could have been carved on both sides). The grooves of each design are filled in with a coat of white paint. The two question stones are distinct from the others, being rather plump, without markings, and of a different stone matrix. When all together, the sixteen pebbles fit nicely into one cupped hand and without much weight. When not in use, they are stored in a light blue, hand-sewn velvet pouch with a drawstring ribbon.

The runestones are cast together as a unit, *never used singly,* as the meaning of each is contingent on its relation to the others. Each cast is directly influenced by whatever forces and energy are present. The cast will always address *the real issue at hand,* regardless of whether that was the question that was asked.

The images that make up a set of Goddess Runes represent the human condition: the masculine and feminine principles within each of us, passion and love, the coming of children and the establishment of families and communities, wealth, growth, learning, positive and negative aspects of choice, the ego, trans-

formation, death. The desire to reconnect with The Source of
Our Being is the basis of their character; truly, they depict the
reconciliation that is possible when parts of a whole rejoin.
Intuition is the equal of intellect in their use.

Symbolically, standing or extended lines represent the male
influence; enclosed triangles or curves, the female.

The following chart illustrates each of the Goddess Runes,
and provides basic key meanings and pebble shapes for each
runic symbol. Traditionally, the shape of a stone needs to "fit"
the rune sign it wears. The shapes shown here, though, are *not*
historical, only suggestive.

GODDESS RUNES

Basic Key Meanings and Suggested Pebble Shapes

Message Carriers

 Boy, man, male, masculinity.

 Girl, woman, female, femininity.

 Love, unity of feelings, harmony, artistic or musical
talent (can indicate sexual passion).

 Marriage or committed union, children, family, grouping of people, community, public.

 Home, house, building, reliability, tradition, practical-
ity, conservatism, discipline, routines, car or mode of
transportation.

 Comfort, ease, pleasure, security, safety, no effort,
peace.

 Confusion, a fog, lack of clarity, a muddle, irrational-
ity, instability, unreliability.

Conflict, war, arguments, anger, difference of opinion, opposition, quarrels, agitation, delays, obstacles, stubbornness, frustration, manipulation, stress.

Negativity, warning, danger, lies, harm, fear, depression, mood swings, problems or difficulties, discomfort, shyness, secrets, worry, jealousy.

Change, movement, a turnaround in affairs, an ending or a division between phases, death, transformation.

Fire, the passion of desire, creative drive, a sense of rightness, psychic ability, spiritual guidance, the future, deity, soul connections.

Beneficial gain, forward motion, improvement, tangible growth, learning, teacher or student, counseling, communications, achievement, possessions, the mind.

Gifts, rewards, promotions, pleasant surprises, good luck, happiness, joy, exultation, extras, expressed or latent talents, flirtations.

Money, finances, salary, work, job, investments, wealth, prosperity, that which multiplies, power, the ego.

Unmarked Question Stones

Female Questioner: stone shaped like a uterus or an egg.

Male Questioner: stone shaped like a penis or a probe.

Enclosed with this book are stickers you can use to create a temporary rune set. You can obtain a permanent set by writing to any of the runemakers recommended on pages 203 and 204, or by keeping an eye out for such offerings in gift shops and bookstores. The traditional way is to gather stones from nature and create your own, so it can be a direct extension of the life energy unique to you.

Should "doing it yourself" interest you, allow your feelings to be your guide. It is entirely up to you how your runes will look and how they will be used. You may use them as a toy, a conversation piece, a game, or as a tool to help you convey a sense of the sacred. It's your choice.

Historically, stone or wood was the preferred material to carve, because each responded well to the carver's blade and was abundantly available. Colors were often added for emphasis, but carefully, by pouring appropriate mixes of dye into each carved groove. Today, an engraver's tool or a wood-burning pen can substitute for the carver's blade, and a narrow art brush can be used to guide the paint into place. Pouches were once tanned leather or furry hides tied with thongs, but today, people often prefer different weights and colors of velvet or brocade, with cording or ribbon used for tying. I once saw a pouch made of fine needlepoint, complete with yarn tassels and tiny bells on the drawstring.

Regardless of how you prepare your set or what you do with it, runes take on "life" only when they are treated with respect. Your set will be little more than a heap of ridiculous rocks unless you put aside all preconceived notions and, like a child, trust yourself to flow with their magic. Rune glyphs are quite capable of teaching you anything you need to know about them. You do not have to second-guess their meanings or enforce any ritualized regimen. Just relax and release yourself from expectations. You need only a feeling of joy and a sense of fun to begin your adventure.

There are some people, like me, who prefer to invoke the spiritual nature of runes. This simply means choosing to hold them in reverence as an extension of the greater good or God. Although the set I work with was prepared for me by another person, it is as if I had put the set together myself; it so perfectly personifies the things I hold dear.

Let me explain.

My near-death experiences taught me that every single thing on earth is alive with a consciousness of its own and possesses a unique intelligence, memory, and responsiveness. Hence, I no longer think in terms of ownership but rather in terms of the enjoyment to be gained through mutual sharing, and the growth possible from life's varied opportunities. Thus, I do not consider the runes I keep as "mine," but rather as "friends." I could no more possess them than I could possess any other life form. Only in freedom can spirit flourish.

Both the fabric of the pouch I use (velvet) and the origin of the pebbles (Mexico) are of special significance for me. When I was a child, many of my dresses were made of velvet, and I would often stroke the plush pile, feeling as if its soothing ripples were a "hug" the dress was giving me. I never outgrew this loving relationship with velvet. Also in my youth, Mexican labor camps were a common sight throughout southern Idaho, with the problem of illegal aliens an unresolved dilemma. This disturbed me so much that I made a point of getting to know as many Mexican laborers as possible, later learning some of their customs and language. Although they lived in distressing poverty, these people proved themselves to be kind, generous, family-oriented, loving, and deeply spiritual. Countless times since then, my life has been blessed by Mexican people and the colorful heritage they celebrate. I feel richer because of this.

This short explanation denotes my particular bias in the creation of a Goddess Runes set, but it also illustrates the need for sentimentality and responsive feeling. In all fairness, though, the runes I share life with have come to mean more than they might have otherwise, because we have grown together, my rune friends and I, as we have explored one another's abilities and potentials.

Even though I now prefer a spiritual approach to anything I do, let me make something quite clear: *we make a thing sacred by the power we give it and by the way we hold it in mind.*

Nothing is sacred by itself, and yet everything is sacred— depending entirely upon how it is viewed and who is doing the viewing. Just because I regard runes as sacred does not mean that they are intrinsically anything other than symbolic glyphs. They are sacred to me because I make them so. You can make whatever you want of them. Should you desire them to be a game or a toy, they will function in that capacity and the magic of their meanings will match the way they are used. Invoking sacredness changes vitality, not validity.

Because Goddess Runes go back in time for uncounted millennia, they are layered with multiplicities of feelings and thought. Each glyph is literally a slice of life captured through the making of its image. Allow your imagination to guide your response to them until deeper nudgings from your subconscious mind begin to surface. You will learn more about *yourself* when you use Goddess Runes than you ever will about *them.*

Goddess Runes are what I refer to as "earthmagic." This means they are reflective, like a mirror, returning whatever is projected. As you seek information about life's many twists and turns, these runes will faithfully illustrate what is *truly* real or false about any situation. They reflect *motive.* Don't forget this . . . how tricky yin runes can be.

Remember, yin runes reveal greater depths of insight than their yang counterparts. One must be willing to risk the unknown in order to use them. Perhaps this is what threatens some people . . . the idea of brushing aside the thoughts that come from conscious thinking so unlimited avenues of the heart can be revealed. The energy that undergirds events and attitudes is illuminated when casting with yin runes. Information gathering is the goal; objectivity is the result. Using them rightly uncovers anything hidden.

GODDESS RUNES

Conceptual Meanings of Each Message Carrier

 Boy, man, male, masculinity: open branches.

The upper half of a man's body was considered the predominant part, as shown by the emphasis on head and arms in this glyph. Man was the provider, the protector, who had great physical strength and knew how to use it. His was also the power to create anew; hence the lower line extension, which came to symbolize an erect penis (assertive projection). According to runic traditions, male energy not only created anew but was the necessary force that "opened up" and "spread forth," as great branches do from tall trees so height can be achieved—whether in sexual encounters, life endeavors/accomplishments, community, or with the Tree of Life in the Germanic/Norse versions of Creation's Story. The whole design is similar to Neptune's Trident (the forked staff), and likewise signaled a love of sea and wind, and a need for freedom. Although man's world was external to him, masculinity was recognized as the empowerment of the self to determine its own separate, independent course.

 Girl, woman, female, femininity: closed roots.

The lower section of a woman's body was given more importance, as shown by the floor-length skirt in this design. In runic traditions, woman was considered the emoter/producer/procreator (the vessel of co-creative power), but notice the upper line extension signifying that woman was the equal of man mentally. The floor-length skirt symbolized the closed vagina or the protected womb, but it also referred to great depths of feeling and emotion. Its shape, the triangle, emphasized a different type of physical strength: the power to endure and make steady, as roots balance the Tree of Life in Germanic/Norse versions of Creation's Story (receptive stability). The whole design is similar to images in other cultures that portray mirrors and the trait of vanity (example: ancient Egypt and Greece). Although woman's world was internal to her, femininity was recognized as the empowerment of the self to bring together in balance and in support for the mutual benefit of the many.

Man and Woman glyphs illustrate the opposite halves of the same whole. Males and females were once considered equally important and given equal status. Neither gender was regarded as superior to the other. In many Celtic, Viking, and older Crimean and Ukrainian cultures, for instance, both sexes had equal rights of ownership and divorce.

Man and Woman glyphs can be interpreted as either singular or plural, depending on how they appear when used in a cast and on what feelings or sensations guide your interpretation.

 Love, unity of feelings, harmony, artistic or musical talent (can indicate sexual passion): the unification of Man and Woman.

Man and Woman glyphs merge in the design for Love to create a single unit, for neither was considered complete without the other. Love in ancient times was most commonly held as the equal and bonded union of male and female energies, joining the qualities of assertive projection with receptive stability in order to forge a whole body complete within itself. Notice that in this design the male penis penetrates the female vagina and claims the womb, hence the idea of sexual love. But more than sex is represented here, for the bonding of opposite yet equal halves results in *true* wholeness. Love was not necessarily equated with passion by our ancestors; quite the contrary. Love was thought to be more of a harmonizing force that created unity, a merging of independent selves within a larger framework. This merger was said to create a support system that would undergird all future endeavors. Rune lore depicts this as the way great trees grow—through the mutual relationship between branches (masculinity) and roots (femininity). Love was recognized as a force that had the capacity to expand or enlarge into something greater than existed before. It is interesting to note that the Love glyph resembles a Native American tipi. Tipis were designed to be flexible and movable, yet strong, stable, and lasting. By its very shape and construction, a tipi is said to automatically accelerate any energy present within it (including that of occupants). The cone shape of the tipi is thought to blend and merge forces in such a powerful way that respect would be promoted and healing fostered. Fittingly, the

tipi design actually personifies what has come to be regarded
as the power of Love.

 Marriage or committed union, children, family, grouping of people, community, public: what results when
Man and Woman (masculine/feminine) come together
in Love.

The union of men and women, or masculine and feminine
forces, brings forth positive results, creating family, children,
and community. Such commitments or marriages secure a firm
foundation for nurturance, safety, and the potential for increase,
including reproduction. Notice that although the children or the
creative outgrowths of the union (represented by the two small
circles, one on either side of the design) were protected and
guided by their parents, they were not considered "owned property." Each egg (circle) represents an independent extension of
the family unit, not chained to or held prisoner by it. Our ancestors understood that once a child was strong enough, trained
and able, he or she must leave the "nest" and seek elsewhere
for whatever life might hold. They also realized that no family
unit was worthy or complete without the bonding that love
provides. This concept was expanded to include larger groupings of people, or the extended family—those with kindred feelings toward one another who might or might not have been
related by blood or marriage. Eventually "family" came to
include the idea of community and the understanding that only
with mutual respect and honor (love) could any group of people
remain together for very long or live in close proximity.

 Home, house, building, reliability, tradition, practical-
ity, conservatism, discipline, routines, car or mode of
transportation: the lower half of Woman detaching
from her body and moving on, the idea that security
can be flexible and not fixed to any particular location.

Dwellings or buildings were often given female connotations in
rune lore, because stability was considered a feminine trait and
the pleasure of hospitality an outgrowth of feminine receptivity.
Thus, structure was dependable, and so was woman as a determined conservator of tradition and worthwhile values. The design, in looking like a woman's skirt or the lower part of a
woman's body, acknowledges this. Notice that the top shape is
a full enclosure, fully protected and private, a sanctuary or
womblike place where one can feel comfortable and safe. The
triangle denotes strength, endurance, and supportive assistance
(even stubbornness). The detached line underneath the glyph
connotes a boat on water or the concept of mobility and transportation. Clearly there is a connection here with Norse cultures,
as the idea of Home includes being either on land or at sea.
Yet long before Vikings roamed, ancient peoples understood
that one's residence could exist in more than one place, sometimes simultaneously, and that "home" was really more of a
state of mind than a fixed location. There is a paradox here—
that stability can be flexible regardless of form, and structure
need not be limiting.

 Comfort, ease, pleasure, security, safety, no effort,
peace: the lower half of Woman extending from her
body to embrace others, the idea that security is now
open to whatever exists beyond structured formats.

This glyph illustrates a state of ease in which little or no effort
is required. It extends the concept of Home and the safety of
a secure and stable environment to include the comfort of joy
and pleasure wherever it might be found. Implied here is a
tradition from many older cultures where hospitality includes
the possibility of sex as a token of good will or as a courtesy.
The importance of feeling safe and comfortable, relaxed and
satisfied, is emphasized. Just as the concept of Home evolved
beyond the idea of a single place or location and came to signify
a more flexible state of mind, so, too, did the idea of Comfort

grow past any attachments to sexual pleasure and came to highlight a more positive and relaxed state of mind. "Easy does it"
best exemplifies this design, which, curiously, when flat on its
side, looks just like a modern-day house slipper or the shape
of someone lying down.

 Confusion, a fog, lack of clarity, a muddle, irritational-
ity, instability, unreliability: the lower half of Woman
divorced from any source of security, an aberration of
the idea of Home; stability is lost—but only temporarily.

Shaped more like a child's set of pickup sticks in disarray,
Confusion looks exactly like what it depicts—nothing is clear,
all points are mixed up or muddled. The confusing condition
of an unclear mind has been described as comparable to suddenly finding oneself caught in a fog or a mist where details
and landmarks are hidden or obscured from view. An individual
can get lost without realizing what is happening. The irrational
construction of this design, plus the abundance of jabbing
points, illustrates that the concept of Home has been violated—
the process of steady, day-to-day living and relating has become
perplexing and disharmonious, even bewildering. Should confusion persist, anxiety and distress can result. The challenge here
is to remember that fog is a temporary condition, easily dissi-
pated by the "fresh air" of a new idea or a better way. Confused thinking evaporates when clarity returns.

 Conflict, war, arguments, anger, difference of opinion,
opposition, quarrels, agitation, delays, obstacles, stubbornness, frustration, manipulation: the lower half of
Woman and the idea of Home are threatened—there
is no way to avoid the confrontation of open conflict.

In this design, the symbol of Home takes on the shape of a
horned battle helmet: precise, pointed, and erect. The glyph also
depicts an individual with feet spread apart in a firm, defiant

stance—all senses alert and combative. The security of Home and the stability of Woman have been threatened. It is time to confront the problem or issue at hand. Negotiations and diplomacy are over. Combative action is front and center—whether that means a disagreement, an argument, a quarrel, a yelling match, an actual fight, or a war. Opposition or an opposing viewpoint undergirds the idea of war and conflict, implying that sides have already been drawn and combatants are ready. Avoidance or delay is no longer effective or recommended. War can be won or lost, but the exercise of "fighting" (facing a problem squarely) is necessary. Because of what this glyph portends, it can also refer to a short temper, temper tantrums, lawsuits, court, jail, crime, hospitalization, degenerative diseases, chronic health complaints, stress; or (if separated some distance from other glyphs in a cast) it can reveal the presence of buried anger from the past, hidden resentment, and/or unresolved issues that are still painful.

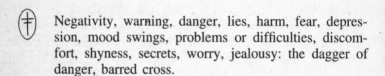 Negativity, warning, danger, lies, harm, fear, depression, mood swings, problems or difficulties, discomfort, shyness, secrets, worry, jealousy: the dagger of danger, barred cross.

The dagger is self-evident in this glyph, with both blade and hilt equal parts of the design. This is a weapon of harm, made to be used either by an individual or against an individual. A warning is intended by this glyph: beware of the dagger's point, for it signifies problems, difficulties, restrictions, or the kind of violence that undermines, discredits, and/or causes despair. Dagger blades in ancient times were often coated with poison, making them doubly dangerous and evil. Even just the sight of one was considered an omen that fortune had turned away and times were ill-favored. Poison could also be administered directly to food or drink. Thus, the potential danger was all the more insidious, as daggers and poisons were easily hidden and disguised. When governments instituted trial by jury, the glyph came to symbolize negativity or negative behavior. This included gossip, slander, lies, worry, cheating, being taken advantage of or put down, accidents, and illness. Today, the glyph is still a warning of uncomfortable times ahead (and, interestingly enough, it is the current symbol for tuberculosis). In a cast, the nature of Negativity can be interpreted by the direction in which the blade points, what it points to, and any other glyphs nearby. Because the hilt shares space with the blade, collusion is implied—not necessarily a secret conspiracy, although that could be the case, but collusion in the sense that there is often a ''connection'' between any given difficulty and the individual involved. This connection is usually indirect or subtle rather than specific, and can refer to unwelcome words carelessly spoken, a faulty decision that put others at needless risk, or activities engaged in without regard to consequences (especially if those activities were the original cause of the negative condition). For this reason, Negativity, like the rune sign for Gifts, illustrates the law of cause and effect.

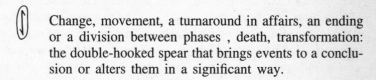

Change, movement, a turnaround in affairs, an ending or a division between phases , death, transformation: the double-hooked spear that brings events to a conclusion or alters them in a significant way.

For a long period of time, barbed lances and spears were used in war. If the initial plunge didn't kill an opponent, then the weapon's removal often did, for the hooks would rip the flesh. The ragged and gaping wound that resulted meant the possibility of mutilation, and/or a painful or lethal infection. These weapons were feared even by the physically strong, and came to be called ''death hooks.'' In this design, the symbol of death is a double hook: there is a barb at each end of the extended line, and the two barbs point in opposite directions. The meaning is clear—death cannot be avoided once an individual's time has come. Ready or not, death wins. As people became more civilized and mature in their thinking, the concept of Death was

altered to denote a time of change when affairs shifted and the
direction of life changed (perhaps a division between cycles/
phases). The hooks came to symbolize the need for action, taking
the initiative to facilitate change. The glyph indicates the idea of
personal growth through transformation. Movement is at hand.
It is time for a change. Although the Change/Death glyph can
indeed mark a physical nemesis, most often it refers to a symbolic ending in one's life: "death of the old; birth of the new."

 Fire, the passion of desire, creative drive, a sense of
rightness, psychic ability, spiritual guidance, the future,
deity, soul connections: abstractions, the unconventional.

Much as flames create spontaneous, all-consuming heat, so passion was considered to be an overwhelming surge of burning
desire. Similarly, as flames can run wild, scorching and inciner-
ating all they touch, so unchecked passion was known to beget
lustful obsessions that could turn destructive. Yet even ancient
peoples realized that passion could also fan the flames of creativity, thus constructively channeling the orgasmic qualities of
heightened sensations and unleashing this power in positive directions. Concurrently, Fire has also been regarded by every
known culture as a sign of deity, containing secrets of the spirit
within its bright-hot brilliance. Passion/deity—the two were in-
separable in rune lore. Note that the shape of this glyph is
angular, bold and pointed, slightly abstract, a chevron. Its
angled design derives from a time when the concepts of Goddes
and the spirit world were beyond the comprehension of mun-
dane society and often at odds with it. Spiritual truths were
received and recognized in altered states of consciousness—
moments when heightened awareness and the ability to exceed
common awareness produced ecstasy, the ultimate passion. As
fire is short-lived, runic traditions considered spiritual inspiration fleeting as well and in need of occasional reinforcement.
The chevron aspect connects the rune sign with birds, high
flight, and the ability to glance the "bright worlds" beyond

earth life; a sense of "future." Interpretations of the Fire glyph
were finally popularized to convey the idea of divine guidance,
philosophy, prayer, spiritual protection, and soul connections. In
some cases, however, the glyph still refers to strong emotions,
unadulterated passion, or the urge to create. A "rightness" of
purpose and an awareness of future "worth" are indicated by
its association with deity.

 Beneficial gain, forward motion, improvement, tangible growth, learning, teacher or student, counseling,
communications, achievement, possessions, the mind:
the consciously directed extension of Fire—progress.

This design consists of two Fire glyphs inverted over each other
in such a manner that extended "tails" spread out behind. The
shape of a fish swimming forward or upward (if the glyph is
turned ninety degrees) is the result. This denotes an addition or
gain in one's life—progress. Throughout rune lore, the fishlike
symbol has heralded a time of beneficial activity when tangible,
consciously directed preparation netted tangible results. Opportunities for learning and advancement were present (whether
in school or by apprenticeship), improvement and expansion
recommended, and acquisitions favored. Since Fire refers to
spirit forces and the concept of divinity, the Beneficial Gain
glyph came to signify a time of blessings as well, when forward
or upward movement was not only appropriate but assured.
Today, we would say "the green light is on" and better times
are at hand. Curiously, this same symbol was once used by early
Christians to identify one another and is still held as sacred by
the established Church. Christian interpretations for this "bor-
rowed" design are not much different from those that have
survived antiquity. The sign of the fish is the sign of nourishment for the body and the soul. Modern-day meanings refer to
the ability to communicate, educate, think and speak clearly,
market, write, advertise, promote; as well as to the art of language, eye contact, ideas, and intellect.

Gifts, rewards, promotions, pleasant surprises, good luck, happiness, joy, exultation, extras, expressed or latent talents, flirtations: Fire touching Fire, good fortune and fun, enthusiasm.

Like Beneficial Gain, this symbol involves two Fire glyphs, only this time their midpoints touch to form an hourglass shape or a large "X." Two spiritual truths are evident in this glyph: the law of cause and effect (whatever you give you receive), and the law of correspondence (as above so below). Grace and forgiveness are implied in Gifts because of Fire's spiritual connotations. Hence, "X" marks the treasure trove. Something good comes or is discovered, and it is deserved. Gifts denotes a time when fortune smiles, happiness is at hand, and pleasant surprises seem to pop up unexpectedly. Rewards are collected; things such as promotions, recognition, accolades, pats on the back, prizes, special favors, and/or objects are freely given. Past efforts undergird these rewards even though Gifts always seems to be something extra, unlooked for, sudden, or by happenstance. Enthusiasm seems to "bubble up"; expressed or latent talents are noticed. "X" was the ancient symbol for "star," the spirit sign of hope and joy, of promises kept and wishes come true, of the awarding of heaven's favor. When an "X" appears as a natural line indentation on the palm of a person's hand, the tradition of palmistry says that it signifies good luck and extra protection. Gifts are pleasures to enjoy—whether they are qualities, talents, behaviors, activities, or objects. A profitable time to gamble or take a risk may also be indicated, as well as fun activities.

⊙ Money, finances, salary, work, job, investments, wealth, prosperity, that which multiplies, power of authority: the seeded circle, a fertilized egg, one's ego.

From earliest times, the concept of wealth was associated with birth and the urge to multiply and be fruitful. Most often, this

was symbolized by a fertilized egg. The design of this glyph
illustrates that idea by showing a seeded circle or a cell body
about to grow, divide, and multiply now that fertilization has
occurred. The creative drive (that urge from deep within the
self) was recognized as the "birthing" force that fueled whatever might manifest; hence, those who produced and/or procre-
ated the most were considered the wealthiest. It didn't take long
for this concept to encompass the fact that one could steal or
falsely possess the wealth of others, thus the emergence of
greed. The rune sign also refers to one's ego and the power of
authority. Modern-day meanings for the seeded circle (moti-
vated inner potential) include the money coin, material gain,
and the activities of finance, economics, investments, and diverse income sources. Employment and salaries are represented
as well. Both astrology and astronomy use this glyph to symbolize the sun, and have since earliest times. As the sun sends
forth its life-giving rays in all directions, so the seeded circle
brings forth and multiplies without limit. Historically, the al-
chemical sign for gold has always been this same symbol, lending even more credence to the potential for abundant wealth
and prosperity that the Money glyph implies.

Unmarked Question Stones

Female Questioner: stone shaped like a uterus or an
egg. Used in casting when a woman or girl wants
assistance.

Male Questioner: stone shaped like a penis or a probe.
Used in casting when a man or boy wants assistance.

Although not runic glyphs, these two shapes are important when
using casting runes. Ancient knowledge was based, to a large
extent, upon sexual connotations and understanding the purposes of and differences between male and female energies.
Maleness and femaleness were considered to be qualities and
activities that were not limited to living beings but were, in

essence, major determinants of how the world functioned. It
was known, for example, that positive energy (male) and negative energy (female) were opposite poles of attraction and as
such were present in all things, whether animate or inanimate.
The explosive energy released during orgasm was seen as a
model for the kind of power it is possible to generate when
positive and negative energies are correctly combined. Realizing
this, early people were able to accomplish feats so seemingly
impossible that, even by today's standards, their methodology
remains a puzzle. The sexual experience, then, meant far more
than merely pleasure and procreation. It was used as a symbol
for the creative power inherent within everyone and everything.
In rune casting, sexual distinctions were clearly made at the
start. For instance, the asking of a question was considered
"male" (outward projection), while the process of answering
was thought to be "female" (inward reception, inner pro-
cessing). Even in the casting process itself, proper energy polarities were established before a single question could be asked.
This was done by using the particular unmarked stone that,
according to its shape, recognized and honored the gender of
the one seeking aid or guidance.

Runic symbols are not magic in and of themselves. Symbols
are illustrative, not directive. The magic comes from the way
they stimulate feelings, emotions, and memories in the one who
uses them. Forgotten wisdoms hidden within the psyche begin
to awaken and resurface. This is the *real* magic . . . uncovering
the deeper depths of your own being.

CHAPTER THREE

The Way of A Cast

CASTING AS DIVINATION

Casting is divining. It is one way of practicing the art of divination, of invoking the invisible, of touching the unknown, of capturing the secret depths a moment can hide by suspending it in time and space. Simply put, casting is a method of throwing or tossing runestones so that they fall in a pattern that provides an illustration of a person's query, your own or someone else's. Anyone can learn the skill. Self-help-oriented, it enables one to seek "higher guidance" (i.e. objective information devoid of emotional undertones).

Divination itself is a universal experience as ancient as it is timely. Most board games, card games, gambling systems, and dice games rely on acts of divination, as do feng shui (geomancy), dowsing, pendulums, tarot, I Ching, and Ouija, to name but a few. Anything that depends upon elements of chance is a type of divination. Any object can be used as a tool in the divinatory process. A stone that is fairly two-sided will do. Just dub one side "yes" and the other side "no" and toss it. The side that lands straight up is your answer, like when you flip a coin.

Practice makes perfect; the more you do it, the more skilled you will become. This practice, by the way, is called "sacred play." Our inner child, that innocent and trusting part of our nature that most of us have tucked away inside our deepest self, easily surfaces when we make a game of learning, when we play. Actually, any type of divination is really no more than a simple, direct, and childlike way of asking for help or seeking assistance from a "parentlike" source of universal knowledge.

Learning the way of a cast utilizes sacred play to help you step into your own "dream" (the life you live) so you can view issues from another perspective. This enables you to develop an ongoing pathway into the heart and soul of your "truthsense," that intuitive wellspring at the central core of all that you are. Once the pathway is developed, you can almost magically move beyond sacred play into a kind of "flow" state where "moment matches mind." This is synchronicity—where random events cease to be random, and seemingly unrelated things link together in meaningful and wonderful ways. The new science of chaos describes this phenomenon by stating that any given part of a whole can reveal the whole; from quantum physics, it is also known that at the subatomic level, everything is connected to everything else.

Rune casting illustrates these scientific findings through the process of "freezing time." From the traditions of shamanism, freezing time means to take a "slice" out of your life and hold it or "freeze" it in your mind as you cast. (A "slice" of life refers to any question or concern you want to focus on; a single issue.) You seek in casting to find *the motive behind the question asked,* not just information about the question. Hence, patterns displayed in the cast will mirror thought *and* feeling, enabling you to freeze or suspend the question asked so that you can examine at your leisure whatever potentials or trends might lie hidden "inside" thought *and* feeling (motives). "Freezing time" is commonly considered a form of "earth magic," whereby one uses natural objects to tune-in on "higher truths."

A flow develops, and you learn to trust that flow. Since there are no formats or layouts in the casting process, you have only your eyes to train and your mind to listen to as the heart takes charge and directs your intuitive responses. There is a grace of bearing and posture that begins to take hold; behaviors relax. As you trust the flow, you trust yourself. As you trust yourself, you become more open to the Source of Your Being, empowered by the power within.

PREPARATION FOR DIVINATION

The word "divination" suggests contact with divinity, implying by its very name that only divine or godlike spirits can respond once invocation is made. *This is not necessarily true.* When you invoke chance, what you receive is chancy! There are no guarantees in the process and no way to know for certain what or "whom" you may have contacted. Practicing any form of divination is like opening wide the inner door to your own subconscious mind. Once that door is open, anything can enter. This can include *any* disincarnate, lower astral being, or whatever "*thoughtform*" (phantomlike substance that appears real) that might be passing by—whether positive or negative in nature. The key to handling this situation is to protect yourself, and the key to protection lies in preparation and intent.

The ancients knew this, which is why they taught stringent and sometimes complicated techniques for self-protection and clarity of reception, often insisting upon apprenticeship through a series of tests or initiations to determine if a person was "ready." They wanted divine guidance, so they practiced divine reception.

Because there has been such a renaissance of interest in runes, all manner of rules, rituals, ceremonies, costuming, sounds, and song are being resurrected, each designed to recreate and reestablish the mystique and mystery from times past. This is fun and amusing. What results is like entertainment, but elaborate extras can make it far too easy to forget what the fuss is truly about.

Preparation for casting is not entertainment, nor should it impress anyone. It is simply a practical way to alter your consciousness and get in the proper "mood." It is a way to center yourself within yourself, to "dust away life's cobwebs" and savor the harmonious, uplifting, positive, and spiritual elements of life. Any form of divination is directly affected by your inner state of mind, regardless of what that might be. Therefore, the more honest and positive your outlook, the more clear and accurate your feedback.

Preparation does not have to be complicated. Whatever it takes for you to quiet your mind and shift your focus within an atmosphere of peace and joy will begin the process. Take as long or as short a time as you wish. I know people who use candles and incense to set the mood, or who just observe silence. Others repeat the "om" chant or do the yogic breath exercise of "A—U—M," verbally intoning each syllable slowly during one continuous outbreath. Some sing. Some pray. Some just relax and smile.

Inner cleansing is also part of preparation. This involves dissolving or releasing negative thoughts and feelings, and replacing them with a focus of love and light. You accomplish this by deciding that you are going to do it, and then actually going ahead and changing what you think and feel.

I have created an audiocassette tape (see page 211) that covers the subject of preparation, and includes a guided visualization exercise that is one of the most powerful I have yet to discover. Shamanistic and mystical in style, the audiocassette is geared to help you stabilize and steady yourself, as your heart is freed to speak and your soul to fly.

A SAMPLE PREPARATION RITUAL

As an example of a preparation ceremony, I would like to share with you what I have devised for myself. I sit upon the floor throughout the ceremony, as this seems more appropriate and feels more comfortable. Before me I spread a white towel, which is used both as a floor cover and as a way to highlight the runestones during casting (and yes, it's easier to wash).

The pouch I use is filled with more than Goddess Runes. Stuffed atop my rune friends, and separated by a sheet of white tissue, are many small objects that put me in mind of sacredness. Having to remove these objects one by one guarantees that I cannot touch any of the runestones until I first alter my state of consciousness. In other words, there is no quick way I can reach the runes. This may seem cumbersome to you, but it has successfully prevented me from succumbing to the force of my own ego. Plus, the relaxed atmosphere created by this ceremony tends to relieve any tension other people in attendance might be feeling, thus enabling everyone to be "four years old again" and see through the eyes of innocence.

I begin the process of centering within myself (inner focusing) by taking three deep breaths and releasing each breath slowly. Next, I begin to empty the pouch, withdrawing from it, one at a time, each object that symbolizes to me a sense of oneness with creation. Often I express out loud what each object means to me as I finger and caress its contours.

Items are removed in no special order. Here is what my pouch holds:

1. A small bell from Bern, Switzerland, which represents to me the unity and interconnectedness of all people and all life-forms.
2. A brilliantly banded, spiral sea shell, illustrating the perfect order of God's creation and the importance of water and the water creatures for maintaining good health.
3. A small wooden egg I dubbed "The Egg of Transformation," which opens to reveal a tiny human form inside. It reminds me that there is freedom of choice. We are never trapped, regardless of our circumstances. We are always free to make new choices and to begin again.
4. A robust, smoky quartz, nearly pitch-black in color, which represents power, energy, and the strength of the Earth Mother we live upon.
5. A fairy basket carved out of a peach pit, which conveys

the importance of our tiny spirit helpers from the invisible kingdoms who help guide form into existence.

6. Two hand-carved wooden angels, each holding a brightly wrapped package that looks like a gift. This reminds me of how confused I used to be about the words "gift" and "talent." For example, one person would proclaim that a lovely singing voice was a gift from God, while another would call that same voice a talent. I spent years studying this paradox, examining it from different perspectives. What I learned is this: a talent is earned or learned regardless of how long it took to do it, maybe even from past lives if you accept the concept of reincarnation; but a gift is a quality, skill, or talent that is so much a part of a person, it helps to define who he or she is—it's like the individual has *become* the gift, perhaps on a soul level. This "becoming," this special part of us, can never be taken away or diminished no matter how many times it is shared. With this in mind, I came to realize that I have many talents, but only two gifts: the gift of joy and the gift of simplicity. Hence, two angels bearing my gifts.

7. A scarab ring from Egypt, which came to me via friends of mine from Turkey. This represents the importance of history, the ancient Mystery Schools, and a value for things past, as history teaches those who are wise enough to learn from it.

8. A Native American flintstone, which was found on Flint Ridge, Ohio—thus, a flint from Flint. This not only salutes the Native American viewpoint, which I honor, but it also reminds me to laugh. Even God has a sense of humor.

9. A stone piece so exquisitely decorated by nature that it seems as if painted by some master artist. It was given to me by a tearful child after hours spent when I helped her and her mother face a painful crisis; she said it represents beauty.

10. Two silver dollars, acknowledging life's abundance, and the fact that money and industry can be just as spiritual as any

other aspect of life. Attitude determines value, not price. The real "bottom line" is service and sharing.

11. A miniature marble from my childhood, symbolizing that the child within is ever present, and ever needful of being nurtured and of being expressed from time to time. A gentle reminder for me.

12. A small yet delicate cameo of a woman, which is an expression of my pleasure at being female in this lifetime and wearing a feminine body. I celebrate the joys of gender.

13. A hand-carved, rosy-pink tourmaline heart within a nest of white tissue. This is symbolic of the heart chakra, the midpoint of energy located in the chest that enables love to flow freely and unselfishly. Because rosy-pink tourmaline is a source of natural lithium (a fabulous stabilizer and balancer), this heart also illustrates how true love actually harmonizes and regenerates all that it touches.

As each object is removed, I carefully place it to my left, where I have laid out white, raw silk napkins from India, embroidered with golden thread and purchased in my youth. These napkins have a multiple purpose. They keep the objects from the pouch separate from the casting area, while doubling as packing material when I store the Goddess Runes in a miniature cedar chest when not in use. (The chest is a place of safekeeping, especially helpful when I travel long distances with the rune set.)

SETTING THE SCENE FOR A CAST

When all the objects are removed, I empty the runestones into my cupped hands and place the flattened pouch on the napkins. Whichever question stone is not needed I put atop the flattened pouch. This leaves in my hands fourteen runestones plus one question stone (either male or female, depending on the gender of the person requesting assistance).

While still holding the runes in my hands, I affirm in silent prayer the protection of God and the privilege each one of us has as an extension of God. I request the highest possible guidance from the light realms and beyond for the individual, affirming divine order in accordance with God's Holy Will. I ask to be of service, devoid of attachment, opinion, or ego. As God is the only reality, I request access to this Greater Truth.

(As a brief aside, I use the title "God" to signify deity. After dying three times and experiencing fully the glories of "bright worlds," I no longer regard God as father or mother, he or she, but join in the chorus of Presence that still sings of God, The One. Should my choice of terminology confuse or offend anyone, I apologize, for such is not my intent.)

I do not allow others to touch or handle runestones, pouch, or symbolic objects that I use. Runes move most easily for me when my energy alone pervades them. They naturally retain a spiritual focus when handled in a sacred manner and kept apart. This is the shamanistic way, a life path that makes sense to me.

My own little ceremony may seem unnecessary to you, but it has proved its worth to me over and over again. Not only does it settle and center me within a cocoon of love and light, but it also has an amazing effect on anyone else present. A special grace seems to envelop everyone, pretense and convention are set aside, and the wonder of childlike joy returns. This happens with Goddess Runes. We return to the beginnings of all beginnings, like some forgotten memory buried in the deeper recesses of our minds.

There are many different ways to employ yang runes. Using the oracle method, one rune is picked from its pouch at random to give you guidance for the day or to offer you another perspective. Or, on impulse, you may pick several of the yang runes. You may also suddenly dump out the entire pouch to see if one or more runes jump away from the rest as if to gain attention. These younger or yang runes can "signal" you by suddenly growing hotter to the touch or by sticking to your fingers as if coated with some invisible glue. This type of runic system actually operates better if used in this oracle fashion, similar to consulting the I Ching, the ancient oracle of China; but it can also be cast utilizing intricate layouts and formats, as with tarot cards. The elder yin variety of Goddess Runes, however, were designed solely for the flow of free-form casting (where all runestones are tossed together as a single unit), and continues the traditions preserved by runesingers for millennia uncounted. Their meanings are based on the interactions of the entire group in a toss, as if they were a community unto themselves whose members "talk" to each other. One member separated from the community has little to "say."

Many times I use Goddess Runes for myself, casting for information about my own questions and concerns. They work just as well for me as for anyone else—as long as I remember to divorce myself (at least while I'm using them) from any emotional investment in the outcome.

Sometimes I demonstrate Goddess Runes within a group situation, casting one question for each person present in turn. Other times I offer private sessions in which in-depth concerns can be addressed. Occasionally I use them for questions from family members or friends. If sponsored, I travel around giving "play-shops," where I help others to discover their own gifts and talents by learning the ancient way of a cast.

Since its inception, I have worked as a rune caster on the nation's largest 900-Psychic-Counseling-Line,[21] and was featured in their first two infomercials (commercials made to look like talk shows) doing live, unrehearsed castings. Yes, what I did was real, no gimmicks. In fact, you may have seen me then, as these infomercials ran continuously, night and day, in every state plus Canada until movie-star versions replaced them. Because of my experience casting on the 900 line, I have come to realize how easy and desirable it is to conduct sessions over the telephone. People tend to be more open if they are safely ensconced in their own homes. Rune casting truly is versatile and without limitation in its use.

PREPARING A QUESTION

I always tell people, the more specific your question, the more specific the answer. However, this is not always the case. I have been asked every type of question imaginable, from the vague and ridiculous to the precise and detailed. Some people labor to phrase their questions in just the right way, while others simply mouth whatever pops into their heads. People will disguise their real questions, beat around the bush, ask "either/or" (which is two questions), indulge in wishful thinking, or confront issues boldly and sincerely. In a group situation, most people are usually too embarrassed or shy to ask the kind of questions they really want answered.

To be honest with you, it doesn't always make that much difference how the question is presented. Runes have a way of answering the "real" question, whether or not it was ever verbalized. They seem to have a mind of their own that is more than capable of knowing what is needed and what isn't. I have seen the runestones jumble up—to the point that interpretation is impossible—when a question seems out of line or somehow inappropriate. Not only can Goddess Runes answer unasked questions, they can refuse to answer any question at all. Runes "know" what they are doing, whether we do or not.

When casting for yourself, the situation is no different. The same advice applies. The catch is . . . be detached and objective. If emotion or need drives the toss (and this can happen when casting for relatives and friends, too), you run the risk of deceiving yourself, seeing only what you want to see. That's why preparation is so important. Your intent must be clear, and open to receive whatever might be shown. A ritual of some kind and prayer can help keep you detached and objective enough to operate from an altered or higher state of consciousness in which your own ego needs have less of a chance of interfering. Honor the casting process—one cast per question is enough. To keep rewording and recasting on the same basic question not only will confuse you with the strange way the runes will seem to behave, it can unsettle your nerves and leave you frustrated.

Should you be unable to divorce your emotional needs from your desire for runic guidance, I suggest that you do one cast on your question, sketch the pattern of the runes after they fall (remembering to label each one), date the paper, then put your drawing away until the following day. Look at your sketch then. It's amazing how clear runic patterns can become after a night's sleep and how wise the guidance is that just seems to "pop" into your head.

Remember, if you cast for another, it is up to the questioner to decide what will be asked and how each question will be worded. Questions are not up to you, unless you are casting for yourself. When others are involved, I request that no question be spoken until I verbally state that I am ready to receive it, and that I be asked only one question per cast. My eyes are closed for better concentration and heightened awareness when I'm casting and I always cast upon a floor, so that the casting space will be unobstructed. Tabletops or laps are too confining.

CASTING

When I truly feel ready, and the one question has been offered for the cast (from me or someone else), I vigorously shake the runes in my cupped hands while repeating the question silently in my mind. I open my eyes, remove the question stone, and place it on the floor in front of me, about midway up the towel. Then I shake the stones again, affirming divine order, and gently toss them up in the air, toward or over the question stone. Each stone lands where it will. Strength or force of throw is learned by trial and error. It doesn't take long to figure out how much force is too much or not enough. Casting has a special "feel" to it, and you will know that feel once you experience it.

I turn over stones that land upside down so that all the glyphs are readily visible. The upside down and backward positions have no significance with Goddess Runes, unlike other forms of divination. I am confident in making that statement because

I have performed many experiments to prove otherwise to no avail. In fact, it would be easier if the glyphs were engraved on both sides of the stones instead of only on one side. Do be careful in turning over any stones, however, as individual positioning in the overall pattern must not be altered.

The pattern formed by casting the stones is more important than the condition of any single glyph. *It is the overall pattern of fall that tells the tale.*

When casting runes, no formats or layout rules are used, for that would defeat the purpose of the cast. Casting involves flowing free of boundaries or limits. To do it successfully, you must learn to trust your own intuition and train yourself to recognize salient patterns.

THE WAY OF A CAST

A Review of Important Points

1. Ask the person requesting aid to silently decide the substance and detail of each question.
2. When you are ready to proceed, verbally ask that person for one of his or her questions.
3. Vigorously shake the runestones in your cupped hands, repeating the question silently in your mind.
4. Remove the question stone and place it in front of you on whatever surface you are using.
5. Shake the stones a second time, affirming that what is most needed will come forth.
6. Gently toss runestones up in the air, toward or over the question stone.
7. Turn over the runestones that land upside down so that all glyphs can be readily seen. Be careful to retain each stone's position in the overall pattern when you do.
8. Study the overall pattern formed by the glyphs around the question stone, using the question stone itself as your starting point and center of focus.

READING A CAST

Casting is different from other forms of rune use, because the technique of freely tossing runes creates patterns within patterns. Each picture or scene making up a given pattern contains many possible variations of meaning. Often, several different interpretations of the same cast are equally valid. The Way of A Cast has no value if you want to concentrate on single glyphs to the exclusion of others, or use runes as an oracle.

As mentioned previously, the key to the interpretation of a cast lies in the pattern of the fall. *The pattern is what free-form casting is all about,* for it reveals the hidden dynamics at play *inside the question.*

The cast illustrates how the stage has been set for each player to act out his or her given role. It shows possibilities and options. It shows relationships. Each cast is valid only for the length of time required to make it. Since we all have free will, anything can change at any time. Nothing is ever fixed. Information revealed in the cast *will not necessarily* answer the question, but it will accurately portray what the questioner is dealing with and the available choices.

Casting is an exercise in objectivity, clarity, and detachment.

There are people who use runes for fortune-telling. But, since fortunes easily change when new choices are made, fortune-telling is a waste of time. Too often, such activity either misleads or misinforms, programming people's minds instead of liberating them. Free will—the right of each person to choose and choose again—should be respected. "Fortune-telling," if truth be known, is a joke we play on ourselves when trying to avoid the responsibility of facing the consequences of our actions.

Learning how to interpret a cast means learning how to speak about what you see, as well as learning how to discern meanings. We are all responsible for how we use language, especially in our dealings with others. People are receptive and inclined to believe whatever you tell them when they are relaxed. A careful choice of words is important. For example, should it appear that runes warn of dire events ahead, do not blurt out that calamity is about to strike. Instead, ask a few questions, prod a little, find out anything pertinent, then emphasize constructive approaches to whatever might seem to be the problem.

Again, remember that the future is never fixed. We may see "shadows" or indications of what might come to pass, but everything in life is subject to change. Even events that seem "fated" can evaporate into thin air when challenged by a new and fresh vantage point.

Sometimes runes are easy to interpret and sometimes they are not. Patterns can be confusing, and we can jump to conclusions or make invalid assumptions. Sometimes what we see for the future is exactly what happens. Regardless of outcome, however, you have *no* right to frighten or try to preprogram anyone. Warn him or her if you feel you must, but watch your words. Warnings can be helpful but, all too often, become self-fulfilling prophecies. The more we think about something, especially in fear or anger, the more assuredly we draw it to us. Responsible speech and positive behavior are worth cultivating, if for no other reason than the fact that life returns to us whatever we give it.

After nearly two decades of casting runes, I have found that I cannot change the patterns they form, but I can change the "eyes" through which I see them. I cannot control what they "say," but I can control what I say.

The easiest way to decipher runic messages is to begin with the question stone and observe how the glyphs arrange themselves around it. Those farthest away from it refer to events farther in the future. Any runes that scoot out of sight during the cast (or off your casting cloth) are not involved in the interpretation and should be retired to the pouch. Any that are bunched together need to remain so, although those that are glyph side down should be turned over (maintaining their original placements within the pile). Spaces between glyphs are important, so be careful not to alter them.

Your vision will naturally tend to move in certain predictable ways once you begin to study runic patterns and interrelationships. There are two primary modes of observation you will use. Your eyes will either seem to trace lines radiating from the question stone or will seem to rotate around this stone, circling again and again as if spiraling. These modes of viewing the stones not only are natural, they are quite necessary. By using one or both modes, you will more easily connect ideas and thoughts with meaning. Undisciplined eyes will search the stones willy-nilly for meaning, missing the patterns or the patterns within patterns.

These two modes of vision are related to the power of image making and the days of our first beginnings. As history has indicated that the star and the spiral are the most universal and most primordial of any designs, it is equally possible that these two shapes have become instinctual response urges that are deeply embedded within our collective subconscious. Whether you agree with me or not, I think you will find as I have that when your vision radiates out from or encircles the question stone, you will pick up accurate information more quickly. Discipline your eyes and you will free your inner vision. Guidance comes from trusting intuition.

Here are some general tips to help you begin interpreting messages from a cast:

1. Always begin by looking at the glyph or glyphs closest to the question stone, and then radiate or spiral out from there. Do not begin elsewhere or jump around indiscriminately.
2. Look for patterns within patterns. There will always be one overall design or theme, but individual glyphs may form peculiar mini-patterns of their own, offering extra information and, sometimes, hidden insights.
3. Notice which glyphs are next to one another. For instance, do all the negative glyphs and all the positive glyphs stay within reach of their own kind, or are they intermingled? Does one type of glyph fence in the question stone, while perhaps another kind encircles it from farther out?
4. Study the distance between the question stone and the runic glyphs, as a way to measure time. All indications of timing

are approximate and based on estimates; however, an inch is usually equal to about a month. Glyphs that are atop or nudged against the question stone are *right now,* or at least of immediate importance. Always measure distance from the question stone outward.

5. Notice the glyph of Negativity. Where does the blade point? Toward the question stone? Away from the question stone? To nothing at all? And what is it next to?

6. Observe the glyph of Change. Does it divide the other glyphs in any way, as if separating or sectioning off groups or creating "phases"?

7. Man and Woman glyphs *do not refer to the questioner,* but rather to other people in the questioner's life (unless there is an identity crisis in that person's life or he [or she] is having a problem with gender issues). Also, the Marriage glyph may not necessarily refer to a wedding or to children. It may symbolize a group of people, relatives, supportive friends (the extended family); perhaps business management.

8. Look for the Fire glyph. Although it once referred to the creative urge and passion, its refined meaning relates to the spiritual life and the spiritual quest, an awareness of deity. For this reason, I consider it a signal of "rightness," showing whether or not a given activity or person is "right" or "on course" for the questioner.

9. Invariably, each cast may be read in several ways. Sometimes the more involved you get as a reader, the more involved the questioner gets, and an in-depth dialogue results. Many times I have read from a single cast for over an hour. Interpreting rune casts is similar to interpreting dreams. There are at least three levels to every dream and sometimes four, corresponding to our physical, mental, emotional, and spiritual natures. Rune use is no exception. The cast enables you to step into your dream, or the dream of another, and view that dream differently. (I use "dream" here to indicate the way life is lived or "the waking dream".)

10. Some runic messages are blunt and short, especially if the individual has asked a yes-or-no question. With these, you find the answer from either a glyph atop the question stone, a glyph next to the question stone, or a certain type of glyph encircling the question stone. Sometimes negative or positive glyphs can make the answer clear by themselves. Seldom is there need for much discussion with yes-or-no questions.

11. Casting about babies and young children often reveals basic character traits, talents, and disciplinary responses ahead of time. This information can be most helpful to parents, and I find it quite satisfying to do. You can also cast for past-life information as readily as you can for the present life. Because this type of casting is so fascinating, Chapter Five is devoted entirely to past-life casts.

12. Rune casting stimulates the intuition. Usually associated with the right-brain hemisphere or the subconscious mind, our intuitive faculties thrive on abstractions, imagery, and symbols—perfect for understanding runic interplays. Intuitive guidance often comes in quick, sudden flashes or strong feelings from the gut. Be open to these responses and give them credence. But remember to include practical logic as well, so your mind can operate from both left and right hemispheres. A whole brain sees all sides to a question, and it can give you a broader range of material to use.

13. The times when you are the most likely to misinterpret a cast are: when you're in a hurry, not feeling well, or allow another to intimidate or overwhelm you. As I see it, each of these situations evolves around the issue of self-esteem (trust) or proper preparation.

When handling runes, remember this fact: they were originally symbolic images and later became hieroglyphs. They were not single words or single letters of any alphabet. The idea of a written language evolved much later in history. Because of this, each picture symbol has a range of meanings rather than clear-cut definitions. It may take you a while to become comfortable with this concept and familiar with possible variations. Runes are very cooperative, though, as they have a way of helping you along by instigating temperature changes or tingling sensations to convey information when you touch them. Various other mannerisms may also be employed to catch your attention. The more you handle runes, the more lively and expressive they become.

If casting sounds complicated, please know that once you begin, it will make perfect sense. After almost twenty years of conducting rune casting playshops, I have noticed that it usually takes the average person only two and a half hours to develop the skill. Someone who is predominantly left-brained may take twice that long, and the average child but fifteen to twenty minutes.

I never will forget the male tax accountant who came to a playshop, insisting all the while that he was wasting his time. After four hours, he suddenly began to cast and interpret like a pro. His mouth fell open, his eyes sparkled, and I swear he was glowing. That man transformed right before my eyes from the argumentative individual he had once been to a man who was happy and relaxed and at peace with himself.

Runes do this to people. They help us to rediscover our true selves.

Just relax, experiment, play, explore.

You'll catch on, too, and quicker than you think.

CHAPTER FOUR

Present-Life Samples to Consider

Developing the skill of rune casting can change the way you use your brain.

After experiencing the radiance of heaven during my near-death episodes, it was rune casting that returned me to the beauty of earth, grounding me back in the world I had left. Learning how to throw and read a cast was the best therapy I could have ever undertaken, as it enabled me to merge the conscious mode of the left-brain hemisphere with the subconscious right brain. The result: in professional testing, I now register as a synergist, with both brain hemispheres functioning more equally and together.

Certainly what happened to me may not seem applicable to you. Yet maybe it is. I say this because I have noticed that those who have been casting a while begin to display different thought patterns. They experience flow states more often (where the brain ceases thinking, "blanks out," while cortical activity increases), develop a heightened sense of logic, think abstractly with greater ease, and conceptualize things in more wholistic terms using *both* brain hemispheres.

I hasten to add here that The Way of A Cast includes more than just casting, though. Tossing stones is tossing stones. It's the *mood* you get into, the way you use your mind, that is so important. Let me explain.

In casting, you don't so much seek answers as you search for that easy, quiet place of peace and harmony within yourself. With "divine expectancy" you trust and feel more than think or analyze. *You allow.* It is an experience in "right feeling," in which the virtue of patience naturally begins to mature as you learn to wait, relax, watch, listen, focus, receive. The human ego can block this process if you hurry or if there are too many distractions, or if you are tired or ill or uncomfortable.

Casting teaches you how to allow the Real Self, the inner you, to surface. It is an exercise in probing the depths of your own being in order to access that pure, clear "voice" of wisdom within you. This sense of knowing is that part of all of us which is nonjudgmental and loves without conditions or expectations. During the playshops I have held, accuracy and breadth of focus improve dramatically for attendees after they have participated in a spiritual ritual of some kind. The only purpose of any ritual, by the way, is to establish a mood that will help align you with The Source of Your Being. Keep this truism central to your casting process and you will do fine.

It seems to me presumptuous to detail page after page of casting instructions; all you would receive would be my own opinion of events out of context from the environment that created them. In order for a cast to be effective, it needs the impetus of the moment in which it is happening and the combined energies of everyone involved. These dynamics heighten perception and enhance accuracy. Under such conditions, needed messages seem to burst forth, as when a petcock is removed to release steam from a pressure cooker. These dynamics are natural and unforced, and they are unique to each particular casting situation. It would be impossible to re-create this kind of scenario on paper. Plus, by overemphasizing my own ideas of interpretive "dos and don'ts," I would risk limiting or stifling your own creative impulses—which are just as valid as mine.

I will, however, share the details of some actual sessions I have had and make a few suggestions about interpretation. I do this with the aim of giving you some samples to consider. Study each sample, noticing the arrangement of the throw and any patterns that are present. Before you read my interpretation of the cast, ask yourself how you would do it. Imagine what you would say to the person who asked the question. Look for several ways to read each throw. *Seek for layers of meaning,* rather than one rigid reply.

Oftentimes I involve questioners in the answering process, allowing them to participate with me in exploring options and alternatives in interpreting a cast. It never ceases to amaze me how quickly the questioner can fit the puzzle pieces together once he or she is given a few hints. Remember, the individual knows his or her life better than you do. Runes are not "crystal balls." They are helpful facilitators of intuitive guidance, and they can inspire your questioner as readily as you.

Right off, make it a point to notice if the entire cast has taken on any particular shape. You can become so involved in the details of what each rune means that you miss the biggest interpretive clue of all—the larger image of the cast itself. As you will soon see, some casts form shapes so striking, just recognizing what that might mean makes any further reading unnecessary. Goddess Runes are *group runes;* they combine their energies to create patterns—it's the pattern you read—and that pattern can be quite large and incredibly simple.

What follows are by no means complete evaluations of the sample casts, but rather, brief outlines of how I work with Goddess Runes and how I arrive at the given reading. There are no set rules to learn besides the general instructions I have already given. Just practice, trust your ability, and experiment. *And don't hurry!*

Note: broken lines and arrows indicate the path my vision took, sometimes spiraling, sometimes radiating out in straight lines, or maybe doing both. How you use your eyes is a necessary discipline in free-form rune casting.

Sample A

In my experience with rune casting, some of the most popular questions asked are: what is the best pathway for me to take during the next six months? Or, what will the coming year be like for me on all levels of my being? The following case focuses on this type of question. A middle-aged woman who had just recovered from a serious illness was contemplating making several lifestyle changes and seeking possible employment. Her question was: "What is the best course for me to take during the next six months?"

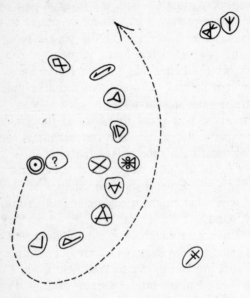

THE CAST

The question stone is female. The long curving arrow shows the spiral vision line I took. Since the Money stone is next to the question stone, finances are obviously the theme of this cast and the woman's greatest concern, although this was unstated. Notice, however, that if you radiate straight out from the Money glyph, you encounter Gifts and Marriage, with Conflict in between them. Next to Conflict is Confusion. These placements indicate that her financial concerns may be of her own making and not a literal fact. The situation in her home appears to be supportive because of Marriage nearby and the overview from

Man and Love. Also, notice that the Negativity rune points to no other glyphs, yet aims in the direction of the past or the empty space below (possibly to the life phase previous to this one). At the top of the runic lineup is Change, bounded by Beneficial Gain on one side and the Love of a Man on the other. She is headed toward making some substantial changes that will be beneficial and will meet with the approval of the man she loves. These key points told me all I needed to know.

INTERPRETATION

Reading from the bottom up, I pointed out that the worst was over and she could relax (Negativity pointing out and down). It was okay (Fire) to think in terms of future changes and employment, but not to hurry. She was still healing and needed more time. I suggested that she might think of some business she could operate out of her home (Home so close to Gifts and Marriage), or some product she could produce there. I advised her that there might be many anxious moments and some arguments about what to do (Conflict next to Gifts and Marriage, plus Confusion), but not to worry, as everything was basically comfortable (Fire and Comfort aligned) and there was a certain rightness (Fire) to the way her life was moving. I spent some time assuring her that money was simply not the problem she thought it was (Gifts near the question stone). It seemed to me that as time went along, there would be a woman or women (Woman) who would offer classes or services (near Change and Beneficial Gain) that she would be wise to take advantage of. At the end of six months (vision line about six inches long), she would be healthier, stronger, and better able to make the kind of changes she wanted. These changes would be blessed by her husband's cooperation and support (Man, Love).

RESPONSE AND RESULTS

As it turned out, the worst was indeed over and the woman's worries about finances were strictly of her own making. What she needed most was rest and recuperation. Because of our dialogue, she began to think seriously about implementing an idea she had had for some time of operating a home for convalescent men (she had never mentioned such an idea during the interpretation). She busied herself immediately after our session with researching proper steps for licensure and legal medical affiliations, instead of wasting her precious energy in needless worry. Her husband was very supportive and, with his blessing, she enrolled in several appropriate classes, all taught by women. The last I heard, she had activated her goal, obtained all necessary licenses, and signed up for her first two boarders—injured veterans from the Vietnam *conflict.* (Notice how her boarders match exactly the placement of Conflict surrounded by Gifts, Marriage, Home, and Confusion. In this case, Conflict was not negative, but representative of the men, like Gifts, who would live in her home.)

Sample B

Love and marriage are topics of eternal interest. This attractive young woman asked, "What must I do to get married?"

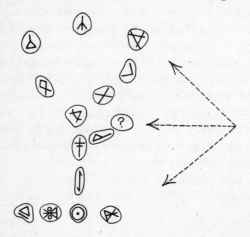

THE CAST

The question stone is female. Arrows indicate my lines of vision radiating from the question stone. This is one of the most unusual casts I have ever done, in that the runes form the exact shape of a chalice (the wedding goblet), with the Man or men in the woman's life suspended over the chalice cup. In a direct line below Man is a lineup of Conflict, Negativity, Change, and Money, with the dagger pointing to Money. Comfort is at variance to the lineup, next to the question stone, indicating an alternative, a way to alter what appeared to me as a deeply engrained habit pattern.

INTERPRETATION

Before I began interpreting this cast, I asked the woman a question: "Do you have a habit of always asking a man's occupation and calculating his earning potential and future worth before you give love and happiness a try?" She became very embarrassed and her face flushed. Her answer was a sheepish "Yes." Needless to say, this reading wound up being a good old-fashioned counseling session on how to form relationships and determine real priorities and values. The key to a change of attitude for this woman was the Comfort glyph, for it showed how love can never be contrived or forced but should always be free to flow in accordance with its own inner timetables. Comfort highlighted the fact that the only real security in life is what an individual feels deep within. External security is but a fleeting illusion compared with the steady stability that comes from self-acceptance and self-esteem. I paid no heed to the other glyphs, for the central theme I had seen was what needed the most attention. Details mattered not. Even if I had chosen to consider the other glyphs, I would have arrived at the same conclusion—it was that obvious.

RESPONSE AND RESULTS

During our lengthy dialogue, the young woman admitted to a long string of failed romances and a brief marriage that ended in divorce. Unrealistic views about money and employment had been at the heart of all her difficulties with men. She lamented about how, during her childhood, her father had drifted from job to job, never contributing much to the family's welfare, and had finally deserted the family. From this early childhood trauma involving her father, she had formed a deep-seated anger and distrust of men. I took the time to teach her several ways to forgive herself and her father, then suggested that if her resentment of men persisted, she would be wise to seek further guidance from a professional psychologist. She appeared visibly shaken, yet excited, when she left.

A year later, after several more failed affairs, she called to thank me for my suggestion that she seek therapy. Even though she hadn't been able to accept such advice at the time, she now realized that I had been right, and she had begun receiving professional counseling. As a postscript, she stayed in therapy for over a year with incredible results: a happy marriage, a wonderful husband, and a bright and playful baby boy.

Sample C

Employment possibilities and the work environment are important issues for most people. During one group demonstration, a middle-aged man, obviously uncomfortable with the idea of rune casting, gruffly demanded, "Should I quit my job?"

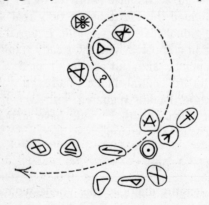

THE CAST

The question stone is male this time. An arrow traces how my eyes spiraled around the cast, beginning at the question stone and the glyph of Confusion. It was plain to me that this man was very confused and upset about conditions at his place of employment (Money is in a lineup with Negativity). He had a good Marriage and family life and the Love of his wife (Woman), but there was definitely a Conflict at his job, specifically related to a certain Man. This Conflict could necessitate a job Change. Such a job Change would involve a major shift in his residence (Home), as well as in his place of employment. Nothing, however, was as clear-cut as his question implied.

INTERPRETATION

Since he was antagonistic toward me and flaunting his aggressive body language, I decided to take a risk with my interpretation and really "lay it on heavy" with this man. In a nonstop, verbal barrage, I made it quite plain that I could not make his decision for him—that the issue of whether or not to change jobs was entirely up to him. I said that in my opinion, however, his problems at work were because of a recent and perhaps continual conflict with a man he had not previously worked with, a man he did not respect and found irritating (Man surrounded by Conflict, Negativity, and Money, with the dagger pointing at Man). I felt that this man must have received his job because of whom he knew rather than because of any personal skill or ability (Gifts near Money). Although the questioner's job was basically a good one, which he probably enjoyed (Fire, Comfort, and Gifts next to Money), I believed he was already considering a possible job change that would involve a physical move to another location (a space between Change and Home/Beneficial Gain, which are to one side). If he took that offer, the move would be beneficial and positive (Home and Beneficial Gain after Change), as his wife and family were very supportive and loving and would do nothing to impede his decision (Marriage, Woman, Love all close together). He would suffer no financial loss regardless of what he did. Both jobs were growth-oriented (Money in line with Beneficial Gain). His question was not, "Should I quit my job?" I informed him, but rather, "Is it worth it to stay and put up with this new guy I can't stand?"

RESPONSE AND RESULTS

I would have liked to have a photograph of this man's face when I was finished. His body instantly relaxed as he sank in his chair. Seldom have I ever been so aggressively confrontational with a questioner, but this seemed to be the only kind of behavior he could respect. He was visibly shaken. After recovering, he described a blatant case of nepotism at his job, in which the owner of the firm had suddenly and without warning placed his own son in the position of supervisor. Not only was the son incompetent, he was arrogant as well, and many employees were up in arms over the situation. For the questioner, it was even more acute, since he now reported directly to the son. He had indeed received another job offer that would necessitate a move. Interestingly enough, this possible move had also appeared in his wife's cast, which I had done just prior to his (although she had asked an unrelated question). The man admitted to attending the rune-casting demonstration that night solely because his wife had insisted he come, but he was now so impressed with the casting experience that he wanted to know more about divination. He expressed an eagerness to pursue metaphysical studies with his wife, something she had been trying to encourage him to do for some time.

To my knowledge, the man is still employed at his original job, but he and his wife have gone on to take countless classes and workshops on human potential, altered states of consciousness, and self-development. Because of what he has learned through these classes, the boss's son is no longer a problem to him. This case is a perfect example of how the Change glyph can also signify transformation. What could have been a job change became instead a change in consciousness.

Sample D

A young man enrolled in college was curious about the coming summer months and the activities he might undertake, so he asked, "Should I move back home and look for a summer job?"

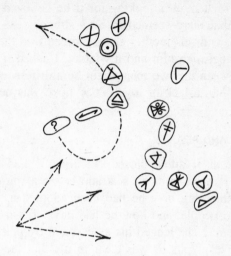

THE CAST

The question stone is male. Several vision lines are indicated. The position of the Change glyph followed by Home and Marriage indicates that this young man had already made up his mind concerning his summer plans. Notice his tendency to doubt and worry about employment, as shown by the position of Confusion next to Money. Also notice a very probable conflict coming up with his father, as shown by the lineup of Fire, Marriage, Negativity, Conflict, and Man. In this conflict, his mother (Woman) would act as mediator between the two (Love and Comfort next to Woman).

INTERPRETATION

I joked with the young man about his question, saying that it looked to me as if his answer was a foregone conclusion. He admitted to contriving the question just to have something to ask. Since summer employment seemed assured regardless of his doubts (Money, Gifts, and Beneficial Gain together at the top of the cast), I advised him to believe in himself and approach the job market with confidence and enthusiasm. He would find what he was looking for if he believed he would. I then noted that there seemed to be a strange sense of conflict in his home, with his mother almost forced into the position of peacemaker between him and his father. I asked if perhaps the problem between the two men might be a difference of personality rather than a lack of love (since Love was next to Man).

RESPONSE AND RESULTS

Suddenly, as if some closed "doorway" had opened, the young man jumped from his seat and began a spirited dialogue with me, explaining how he had been adopted as a youngster by these two people, and how he had never felt truly loved by either of them. I challenged his assessment by pointing to both Fire and Love glyphs. It was clear to me that the family relationships were based on mutual affection, strong bonds of kinship (Man, Love, and Woman in a horizontal line), and spiritual unity (Fire as the lead rune in a vertical lineup, next to Marriage). I reminded him that biological parentage does not necessarily make anyone a true father or mother with sons or daughters. Family titles are earned, not automatically conferred. He then confessed that earlier years with his adoptive parents hadn't been so bad, but now that he was in college, he and his father argued all the time. I asked him to describe how the two of them battled and what they battled about. During his animated reply, I perceived several areas of tension that would benefit from an objective viewpoint offered by an individual not involved in their relationship. With this in mind, we spent the rest of our time together discussing the art of positive conflict resolution and methods for handling anger constructively. I was able to illustrate for him how he was just as much to blame as his father for their recurring quarrels, and how he could take the initiative in redirecting that energy into more practical channels. He seemed puzzled at first, then excited about the ideas I had presented. He vowed to make some changes—beginning with himself.

Sample E

Occasionally I experience a cast that is so dramatic, it is unforgettable. This one involved a woman who looked far older than her years, was critically overweight, and was barely alive from a whole series of health problems including a heart attack. Her doctor had just released her from the hospital. She was well known in the community for her unselfish generosity and her willingness to lend a helping hand to others. She was also an inspiration to many for having successfully surmounted a number of personal tragedies and setbacks in the past. Now, when faced with the toughest health problem of all, she asked a surprisingly blunt question: "Should I go ahead and die?"

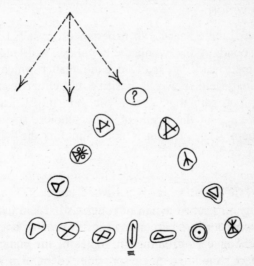

THE CAST

The question stone is female, and radiating vision lines are shown. Notice that the rune for Negativity is not in this throw. It rolled far out of sight and was retired to the pouch. The amazing part of this cast, however, is that Change (also known as the Death glyph) landed straight up on its end and remained in that unusual position throughout the session without falling. The floor was carpeted, but not in a shag or any kind of bulky weave that would enable a stone, especially one that is so long and narrow, to stick straight up. The carpet was, in fact, quite smooth. Never before or since have I seen anything like it. It was almost as if that particular glyph was held erect by some unseen hand.

Pay special attention to the arrangement of the stones in a perfect triangle with the question stone as the uppermost point. Also notice that Love is on a second corner of the triangle and Fire (spirituality) is on the third corner. Because the overall pattern is so dramatic, the other individual glyphs seemed unimportant to me.

INTERPRETATION

Having had three near-death experiences myself, I felt qualified to respond to the woman's bluntness with more of the same. I simply said, "It really doesn't matter which way you decide, because either way is positive and either result will be beneficial. You gain if you stay, you gain if you leave. There is no difference in the result of either choice, so you decide between them. The question is not, 'Should I die?' but rather, 'What do I do about me?' "

RESPONSE AND RESULTS

The woman breathed a sigh of relief, as if I had just released her from some terrible burden, and the two of us began a very powerful dialogue confronting all angles of the choice she felt she must face. She knew of my previous encounters with death and, because of that, felt at ease to unload her own deepest thoughts and feelings. As it turned out, she was "weighed down" with an accumulation of repressed guilts, fears, and heartaches from decades of forcing herself to appear strong and capable of handling anything—a veritable Rock of Gibraltar.

These repressed burdens, it seemed to me, accounted for her large body size. Since her life pattern was similar to mine, I had no difficulty responding to her. My son had once personally toured the famous Rock of Gibraltar, so I could share with her that the Rock was hollow and, like the Rock, our unrealistic desires to be superhuman were equally hollow. This statement caught her attention. Needless to say, our conversation lasted for several hours, and I swear she looked younger and lighter when we finished. Her choice, by the way, was not only to live, but to live life with a fullness and honesty she had never before experienced. This pleased me deeply.

Sample F

Some questions are so complicated and so outlandish that it seems as if it would take a miracle for fourteen little runes to have anything worthwhile to offer as a response. One such question was put to me by a man in his early thirties. He described a piece of land near a well-traveled interstate highway that he and several friends wanted to develop as a tourist attraction. He pulled out a large map and showed me the general location while he continued to describe their idea. He noted that the exit ramp from the interstate led to a short access road that ducked under a bridge and then up a slight rise to a special mound of earth said to be sacred in the Native American tradition. Trees grew to the north of the mound, he continued, but the mound itself was barren. Their plan was to turn the access road into a posted footpath. This would be supervised by guides who would explain to visitors the various markings in the area and the importance of the mound. His question was this: "What kind of signs should be posted on the footpath?"

THE CAST

The question stone is male. For some reason, my eyes did not flow to the Fire glyph after Confusion. Intuitively, I was drawn to jump from Confusion to Negativity and to read the

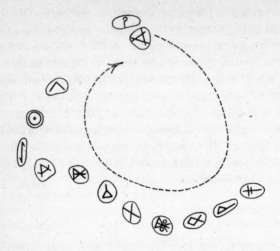

glyphs in a clockwise spiral fashion, one by one, ending with Fire. Runes for Man and Home are missing because they jumped far away from the others during the cast and were retired to the pouch. Confusion reigns in this toss, with the remaining stones lining up in a serpentine manner; yet my gut response to the even spacing between them was that each stone stood alone as a separate and distinct entity not contingent upon its neighbor—while still part of the same story line.

INTERPRETATION

To my surprise, the runes seemed to respond to this difficult question by forming a "footpath." From this design, I was able to outline eleven places on the proposed walkway for tourists where either signs could be placed or stops on a lecture tour could be held. Reading from the bottom right upward, here is what I suggested to the questioner: (1) Negativity. This would be the staging area, where guides would meet tourists. Chances are most tourists would be tired, hot, perhaps grumpy, and not necessarily interested in any kind of sightseeing that entailed personal effort, especially outdoors without protective covering. (2) Comfort. Here the guide would be faced with "winning over" the visitors, instilling in them a sense of curiosity and enthusiasm, and putting them at ease. (3) Beneficial Gain. At this point the guide could emphasize the historical significance of the area and the benefits of experiencing it in this unique fashion. (4) Marriage. Here, the family life and traditions of Native Americans could be highlighted. (5) Gifts. Participants could be invited to think of something they could give during a campfire ceremony at journey's end, perhaps a stone they had picked up or a pinecone, maybe even a song or a poem. (6) Woman. An explanation could be given at this spot about the Native American belief that the earth is alive and is our "mother" in the sense that she provides nourishment, support, and protection. (7) Love. Here, comments could be made about the Native Americans' sense of sacredness with all things (love and value) and how this was expressed in their lore. (8) Conflict. Today's more materialistic views of "me first" and "to hell with nature" could be compared at this point with Native American views of respect and honor. (9) Change. At this spot, a campfire could be previously prepared for the performance of a short ceremony in which participants could, one at a time, offer their gifts to the Great Spirit. They would be giving in order that they might receive, releasing in order that they might be filled anew. (10) Money. The ceremony could end with comments on the Native American philosophy of sharing the wealth and working together as a team to enrich the whole. (11) Fire. At the mound's base, there could be an invitation for visitors to sense the sacred power of the spot, and the specialness of both the place and the moment. A brief talk might be given on how worship and spirituality are an integral part of Native American life.

RESPONSE AND RESULTS

When I finished elaborating on the sign suggestions, the man pointed to an enlarged relief map and noted how the "footpath" created by the runic cast corresponded exactly with the physical shape of the access road. The points I suggested excited him and started a flow of ideas. Remembering the position of the Confusion glyph, I cautioned him about practicalities such as land use and zoning laws, regional park authorization, and regulations controlling historical sites and their development into tourist areas. I advised that a large cash outlay would be needed, especially for advertising and promotion. Although I felt he was being unrealistic in his aims, it was obvious that he was genuinely inspired and enthusiastic. Without discouraging him, I continued to emphasize caution.

A year later, the project folded. The questioner had gone to court to stop a proposed sale of the land to a commercial manufacturing company, and was roundly made to look foolish in newspaper headlines. In the end, new jobs and increased revenue won out over park preservation, especially after the media revealed that the man could not authenticate the site historically. As you can well determine from this cast, runes did not predict any future existence for the park. All the runes did was supply information related to the question asked. This information was based on the potential of what *could* happen, not necessarily what *would*.

Sample G

A middle-aged couple had moved to a new town because of promised employment, only to discover four months later that the job situation was not as claimed. Faced with mounting bills and less income than expected, they asked: "Should we drain our savings account to pay off our debts?"

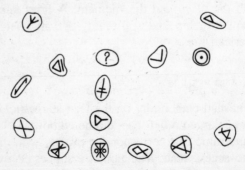

THE CAST

The wife spoke for the couple, so I used the female question stone. No vision line is indicated because, in my opinion, the answer was cut-and-dried and needed no interpretation. Can you see why? Notice where the dagger of Negativity points. In addition, the overall shape of the cast looks like an "A," representing "Account," fallen over and exhausted.

INTERPRETATION

I looked both people straight in the eye and answered, "No!" This reply was so plain to me that I did not bother interpreting any of the glyphs.

I did a whole series of castings for this couple, and in each and every one of them the same basic patterning appeared, regardless of the question asked. This phenomenon is commonplace, for if a certain message needs to be delivered, it will repeat itself over and over again (as if the runes are "nagging"). To illustrate this, here is one more cast done for these people. Pay more attention to the pattern than to the actual question, then compare it with the prior cast. The question this time was: "What is our immediate future in this town?"

THE CAST

The wife again asked for the couple, so the question stone is female. Notice, however, that the cast is divided into two different sections. The vision line for the pattern of immediate importance spirals around from right to left, beginning with the Fire glyph, but another major alignment toward the top of the cast conveys an overall or future message. In comparing this casting with the previous one, notice that in both casts Fire is close to the question stone, and Home is near Change and aligned with Woman, Love, Marriage, and Gifts. Many times I have had glyphs divide themselves as they have here, forming separate messages or themes, and sometimes even addressing

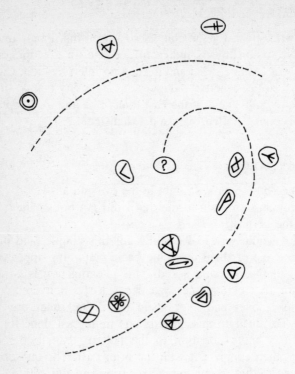

different topics or questions. This time, the message of the upper section is clearly stated.

INTERPRETATION

Since the couple were obviously worried about the wisdom of their recent relocation, I took the Fire glyph's consistent positioning near the question stone as a signal that their move was okay—that they were not to regret what they had done. Living conditions were comfortable enough and the husband was learning a great deal on his job (Beneficial Gain, Comfort, and Man together), even if his income was less. We talked about choices, and how it is that even decisions that appear ill-advised can sometimes either lead to other important moves or prepare one for other experiences that lie ahead. After making this point, I stated that it was my sense they would move again, probably in three to four months (Change three to four inches away from the question stone). But this second move would not be ordinary, in that conditions surrounding it would be confusing and unclear. Once they had moved, however, conditions would be better (the vision line ends with Gifts). In recognizing what looked to me like a warning concerning their future (the top lineup of Negativity pointed at Conflict and Money), I felt a need to be openly honest and simply say to them, "There is no money to be made where you are now without the constant presence of negativity and conflict."

RESPONSE AND RESULTS

The couple seemed resigned to their fate, as nothing seemed to be working for them no matter what they did. Even though their rental house was the nicest place they had ever lived in, and the area was a delight, both of them felt out of step, as if they didn't quite fit in where they were. Previously, they had invested five years in jobs that had been successful but had offered no future. Mired in the rut of complacency, they had been forced into action only after their previous landlord had sold his entire apartment complex. A wonderful job offer had then brought them to this new town, but the job had turned sour. Company management was too demanding and inconsistent. Many employees, not just the husband, were leaving the company. Both husband and wife were busy looking elsewhere for work and were willing to move if something better could be found. This second move, by the way, showed up in seven castings, with the same runic glyphs at the same distance from the question stone in each casting!

Three years later, I was puzzled to learn that the couple had stayed in town. On inquiry, they explained why. Sure enough, four months after our session, with no jobs to be found, each had seen the need to take drastic action: he obtained temporary employment several hundred miles away, and she went on a public-speaking tour throughout New England. Leaving their

rental home intact, they got by as best they could by renting
rooms wherever available. Eight months later, they returned,
paid off their bills, found steady employment, and continued
with their lives as if nothing had ever been disrupted. This new
employment, however, hinged on their abilities to calmly handle
the strains and pressures of constant challenge—he as the new
manager of a radio station embroiled in the chaos of previous
mismanagement and internal conflicts, and she as a nationally
published author on controversial subjects. In facing what had
once seemed a bleak future, they had made peace with the
negativity of fear and anger and were now in demand for their
problem-solving abilities and inspirational leadership. Both
claimed that the rune castings I did for them were helpful, as
the information given enabled them to take the initiative in
altering the outcome of their lives by making different choices.

What had seemed to me like a dire warning about their inability to make any money without the constant presence of negativity and conflict (the top lineup of Negativity pointed at Conflict
and Money in the second cast pictured) turned out to be the
"piece of advice" they used to good advantage. The "warning" clarified for them *exactly where they could make money,*
so they looked for just that, and found prosperity and success.

Sample H

An unmarried man three years into what appeared to be a
thriving career in hairstyling asked: "Will I be able to purchase
a new automobile this spring?"

THE CAST

The question stone is male. Vision lines radiate. Love and
Confusion are not part of this throw, as they scooted across the
floor away from the cast and were retired. At first I involved
myself more in studying individual glyphs than in looking for
overall patterns, and by doing this, I almost missed the most
important clue of all. As with dream interpretations, runic messages may sometimes be misread if you spend too much time

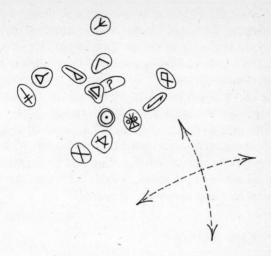

concentrating on details. It seemed clear that in this cast the Home glyph could symbolize the man's hoped-for car (plus it looked and intuitively felt like the car in question). Because of Fire and Comfort, it appeared as if there would be no real problem securing the car, although Conflict next to Money made it plain that price would be a factor. I also noticed an indication of a possible job change, probably beneficial, which would be a factor in buying the car by spring (Marriage, Change, and Beneficial Gain close to Money and the question stone). There are many layers of meaning in this cast, plus one large, overall statement. I almost missed this one, and had to reread it three times before I caught on. Can you recognize what I tended to ignore?

INTERPRETATION

First of all, I reassured him that he could indeed procure his car by spring (three months away) if he truly set his mind to it. There was nothing really holding him back except probably cash in hand versus the price of the car (Negativity pointed away). Then I looked further and began to talk about his job

(Money) and how it seemed to me that his money base could change (Money, Marriage, Change) even before spring (Change less than three inches from the question stone). This could bring with it a new place of employment and many doubts and conflicts over money (Beneficial Gain, Change, Marriage, Conflict, and Gifts, all in alignment with Money in the middle). Somehow, though, all would turn to his advantage. Worry was not needed (Fire next to the question stone). Connected to this situation was a woman who seemed troublesome but really wasn't (Negativity on one side of Woman, Comfort on the other). Also, a man might come to his aid—someone who was like a mentor (Man above Fire and somewhat removed).

RESPONSE AND RESULTS

The hairstylist had already picked out his dream car and was actively engaged in a loan search before he came to me. We began an animated discussion about choices, goal setting, and various ways in which he could make his dream come true. He admitted to feeling restless at work, as if it were time for a change. The more we talked, the more open he became, until he finally confessed to having accepted new employment two days before. Construction on the new salon was delayed, but he wasn't worried since financial guarantees had been substantial. As I listened to him, I got nervous. Either this man was playing with me because he was distrustful, or he was gullible or naive. Nothing felt right. Something was missing—a link, a cohesive thread tying together the various glyphs—and he was no help at all. What was it? I took a deep breath, allowed my vision to blur in relaxation, and looked at the cast again. Details faded and the missing clue (the overall pattern) revealed itself. Yes, the cast looks like a large "H," but what else does it look like? A square! Immediately I changed the dialogue. I said, quite frankly, he was kidding himself about the car. He was literally *boxing* himself in with rigid presumptions and fixed ideas that had nothing to do with the reality of his life. While challenging him, I asked, "In light of your question, what does a square mean to you?'' He answered that a square symbolized to him an economy model car or a used car (his dream had been a flashy racer with a price tag of five figures). ''Is that all?'' I continued. ''Uh, well,'' he began to stammer, ''how about stubbornness?'' A smile crossed my face as I recognized the flush of red in his. As kindly as possible, I cautioned him to forget the car for now and concentrate on his new job. The casting indicated to me that all was not well, that there could be many problems and many delays with the construction, and that even once the salon opened, the financial guarantees might not be honored. ''Hold on to your money and practice conservatism,'' I advised (square/conservative).

Six months later, he telephoned. Construction delays had been incredible. There had been four months of them, forcing the new salon to open in an off-season. Guarantees had been canceled. What had at first seemed to be negative confrontations with both his former employer and his new one (both women) turned out to be positive opportunities to clear the air and settle grievances. Because of my advice, he had scaled back expenditures and had managed to outlast the ordeal. The new job, however, proved to be worth waiting for, and it included the side benefit of a management training program provided by the salon owner, a man who became like a mentor to the questioner. The car idea was abandoned in favor of debt payoffs. ''I will get the car someday,'' he said with a laugh, ''when I am truly ready.''

Sample I

A successful, middle-aged woman was concerned about her career. Hospital administration was her field, but in order to achieve her goals, a Ph.D. degree would be necessary. With this in mind, she asked her question in two parts. First she asked: ''Should I enroll in the Ph.D. program offered at my present location?''

THE CAST

It felt better this time to allow my focus a counterclockwise spiral flow from the female question stone. With all the positive

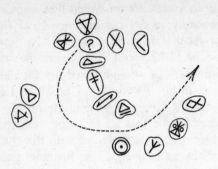

glyphs surrounding the question stone, notice that one of them is Confusion. Off to one side are Woman and Conflict, but pay special attention to the curving lineup of runes beginning with Negativity.

INTERPRETATION

It seemed appropriate for me to be businesslike with this business question, so, without fanfare or hesitation, I began talking. Yes, she would like to stay and take the required courses locally (Comfort, Gifts, Love, and Fire next to the question stone). It would be very comfortable, convenient, and enjoyable, and she would like the people in the program very much. But no, I would not recommend signing up. There was a significant chance she would receive a job offer elsewhere and move, making it difficult to complete the local college classes once she had started. Plus, I was uncomfortable with job offers in general for this woman (Negativity pointing to Change and Money), as she was so undecided about the whole issue. I mentioned the possibility of an argument or conflict with a woman before any move or decision about her future was made, but that this would not be connected to her business; rather, it would be an isolated event (Woman and Conflict to one side). What continuously bothered me about this woman and her focus on obtaining a degree was that Confusion was the closest rune to the question stone.

Her second question concerning this issue was: "Should I enroll in another Ph.D. program wherever I move?"

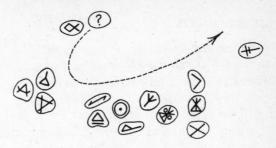

THE CAST

Again it felt right to allow my focus a counterclockwise spiral flow from the female question stone. It seemed to me that this cast was divided into three parts: the answer to the question (as defined by Beneficial Gain next to the question stone), the isolated Conflict with a Woman (Conflict, Woman, and Confusion to one side), and the abundance of glyphs after the Change stone. Negativity seemed not to be of importance because it pointed up and away, yet it signaled to me that this question was not quite what it appeared to be, since the stone was the last of the glyphs.

INTERPRETATION

This cast confirmed the earlier one. It indicated to me that a move was a foregone conclusion for this woman. But I again urged her to wait, to reassess the Ph.D. programs after she was certain where she would be living and what she would be doing. I sensed that her future looked ripe with definite promise and a multitude of opportunities and choices, including satisfying relationships with men, more job satisfaction, excellent learning opportunities, and career advancement. The conflict with the woman seemed unavoidable, but it was probably insignificant, since no other glyphs were involved. It would most likely be an argument of some kind, or a difference of opinion.

RESPONSE AND RESULTS

The woman perked up and her eyes gleamed. She had withheld the fact that she had already received five excellent offers of employment elsewhere, all paying substantially more money than she was now making. She had delayed making any decisions about these offers because the local Ph.D. program was headed by a man she enjoyed being with and respected highly. Several of her friends were also enrolling in the same program, making it even more difficult for her to make up her mind. She admitted to finding the whole situation very confusing. The casting helped her to admit the obvious—that she was not happy where she was and that she was more than ready to make a move. She realized that an advanced-degree program should not become a stumbling block in her pursuit of more challenging and exciting opportunities elsewhere. She would actually limit her future, not enhance it, by staying where she was—an important realization for her. The castings gave her "permission" to do what she wanted to do in the first place. Her comment told me that her real question had nothing to do with a Ph.D. degree, which had been indicated by the strange position of the Negativity rune—last in line, going nowhere. Her problem was low self-esteem. She didn't believe in herself. What began as a rune casting became a session concentrating on her extensive skills, training, experience, and accomplishments—plus the magic of self-confidence. What she needed most she received—a big hug and a pat on the back. She left smiling from ear to ear.

Sample J

The following example is another love-and-romance question, only this time it was from a middle-aged woman who was divorced and had two grown daughters and a young son. She asked: "What is the future of my relationship with my new boyfriend?"

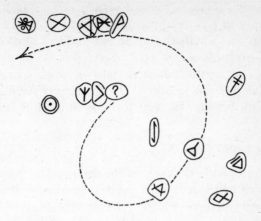

THE CAST

The question stone is female. It took me a while to decide how to view the cast, but finally everything made sense when my vision line flowed in a spiral. Again the runes arranged themselves in three sections, but intuitively I felt these sections to be past, present, and future. The present group is next to the question stone, the potential future group is above the question stone, and the past group is at bottom right. Notice that the first two groups have their glyphs lumped together, while the bottom-right glyphs are far apart.

INTERPRETATION

It looked to me as if she had found Mr. Right (Fire and Man next to the question stone). Although it was not clear at this point, the relationship could easily mature into a comfortable love affair culminating in marriage (Comfort, Love, Confusion, Gifts, and Marriage in a row). However, there was a problem, and it might wind up being the deciding factor. Notice that Change is like a wall or curtain separating one section of the cast from the others. My feeling was that the bottom-right glyphs referred to the boyfriend's past, not the woman's past. Therefore, the unresolved question was—could he release his past hang-ups about women? I sensed that he had been hurt quite deeply in past relationships (Negativity pointing directly at Woman and Conflict) and he still carried unresolved pain, fear, and probably anger as a result. This could prevent him from any meaningful coupling, now or ever. I urged her to be cautious and not to hurry. The future was only a potential (Confusion), but the past was real and in need of healing.

RESPONSE AND RESULTS

The woman nodded slowly as she described his previous marriage, which had indeed been painful. Apparently it was a particularly ugly divorce which had cost him dearly. Because of this, he shied away from even the mere mention of commitment, let alone marriage. Yet the two of them had fallen deeply in love almost immediately and could hardly stand to be parted. She loved him, but she was realistic enough to understand that love alone might not suffice. We talked for a while about how some people prefer to retain painful memories as handy excuses to avoid taking future risks. The possibility of another failure can outweigh the equal possibility of a new success.

A month later, the woman called me long-distance and related a slightly different tale. The man had actually been reticent about commitment because he had been living with another woman all the time he had been seeing her. He and the other lady argued constantly, so he decided to leave her. He had assumed that my client knew about the other woman, when in truth she had not. Since the man had ended his relationship with the other woman of his own choosing, the questioner had no problem accepting the situation. This both surprised and delighted the man. He and the questioner are now dating regularly.

I mused about the turn of events and went back to my notes to study the drawing of the cast again. Had I been more alert, I could easily have seen that it wasn't necessarily *past pain* and difficult memories holding him back, but rather a very present live-in lover. I felt foolish for not having recognized what was going on sooner, and I wondered why the terms "past" and "memories from the past" had felt so applicable at the time. The idea had fit, yet it didn't fit. I had bypassed an important "other layer" to the cast by "taking off" on the tangent I did. My original advice turned out to be sound, however, and at least for that I was grateful.

Sample K

Love can take on many forms, including a few that are unexpected. Illustrating this theme is what appears to be a typical question from an unmarried woman in her late twenties. She asked: "When am I going to marry?"

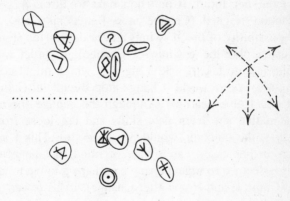

THE CAST

The question stone is, of course, female, and my eye focus radiated rather than spiraled. There are two separate issues and two different time frames in this cast, almost as if two questions had been asked, not one. One section of the cast curves up and is complete within itself; the other curves down and is equally complete. Notice Comfort next to the question stone and Confusion next to Fire. Change is atop Beneficial Gain and in perfect alignment with Love, Woman, and Money in the section below. Marriage skipped off and is not part of this casting, alerting me to the fact that the question of marriage was not the *real* concern of this woman.

INTERPRETATION

The theme of this casting is complacency (all top glyphs are positive ones in an easy arrangement with Confusion next to Fire), plus the problems inherent in being too comfortable (Change atop Beneficial Gain and, next to Comfort, the closest to the question stone). I told the woman so. All was well and all was right (Fire and Gifts near the question stone), except for the fact that the woman was unhappy (Confusion between them). Life was good, she was on course (Fire), but there were doubts about her future (Confusion next to Fire). A growing dissatisfaction reigned (Change atop Beneficial Gain), along with the possibility of mood swings and/or depression (Fire next to Confusion plus the position of Change). In order to grow she would have to take a risk, a big one, which might compromise her safe, secure world (Change atop Beneficial Gain (with Comfort and Home nearby)). Although the change she needed necessitated that she learn new skills and cut loose from her old lifestyle, the outcome would be successful. This I assured her. Fear, in her case, was a state of mind, not an actuality. The casting seemed to urge a change, perhaps a move to another location (Comfort and Home after Change). If the lower section were considered a reference to the man she wanted to marry, then he was quite busy tending to his own problems, which seemed to consist of a love commitment that was dying amidst quarrels, feuds, and anger (Man, Woman, and Love fenced in by Conflict and Negativity). The core issue of his contention was, in all probability, financial, hinging on money and possessions. Although no resolution to the man's quandary was in sight, it appeared that if the questioner moved to this man's vicinity, it might make a difference (Change and Beneficial Gain aligned with Love, Woman, and Money). This was a big "if," though, and with no guarantees. But should the lower section be regarded as a business signal rather than a possible love interest, then she might indeed be moving far away from where she currently resided, to accept a better-paying position and a happier life. A woman's loving friendship would make a tremendous difference in making the move. There might be problems on the job, but nothing she couldn't handle (Negativity pointing down and away), and her new boss would probably be a man.

RESPONSE AND RESULTS

The woman's eyes grew wide as she expressed surprise at how accurately I had described her situation. She confessed to having signed up the day before for psychological counseling to help her deal with increasing depression and mood swings. The same day she had also registered for skill-improvement classes. She was restless, yet she felt imprisoned by what seemed to be a life so secure that she dared not change. Her phrase was, "I'm stuck in a rut." The idea that the man she wanted to marry might also be stuck came as a balm of comfort, reassuring her there was no need to hurry, for he wasn't ready either. Whether or not any love affair was truly in her future, she was the most excited about the prospect of a move and a new job in another area.

A year later, a friend of hers called and told me that the woman had indeed moved, after completing counseling sessions and becoming certified in new job skills. It was the friend who called who had made the move possible. Apparently these two women had known each other since childhood and were like sisters. And yes, there were problems at the questioner's new job involving petty quarrels among the staff, but they were nothing of real consequence. Her new boss, a man, was exceptionally kind and easy to work for. The casting had helped. It had given her courage, plus the will to change. Regardless of whether this questioner ever finds the man she wants to share her life with, she became further bonded with a dear friend, and discovered in the process the right to claim her own future and her own worth without fear.

Sample L

Life can sometimes bring harsh choices. This attractive but plumpish woman in her early thirties was born with a deformity that had necessitated multiple surgeries over a stretch of many years. She was recovering from yet another round when she asked: "Will I have to face major surgery again on my left leg at any time in the future?"

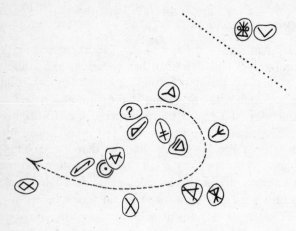

THE CAST

My eyes automatically spiraled clockwise from the female question stone and, in so doing, my first impression was that the casting had nothing to do with her question. The possibility of future surgery wasn't what was bothering her, but rather, the situation in her home involving her husband, her job, and their finances. Study the casting. What do you suppose led me to that conclusion? Notice Man, Love, and Confusion creating an uncomfortable Home situation, and that Marriage and Fire are far away in some distant future. The dagger point of Negativity directly impinges on her sense of comfort, security, and being appreciated. Normally, I do not consider the Woman rune a reference to the questioner, but in this case I made an exception because no other woman was involved (I asked), plus she seemed to lack any form of positive self-image. (Thus, Woman in the sense of an identity was at risk, as clarified by the dagger point of Negativity.)

INTERPRETATION

I wasted no time and minced no words here. These two people, the woman and her husband, must have been having difficulties for some time (Confusion next to Love, with Fire and Marriage so far away). This caused me to become suspicious of how long they had been together and why they had married in the first place. Common sense also told me that surgery costs had probably "tipped the barrel" for them financially, thus compromising their financial security (Conflict atop Money). But with Gifts nearby, and with Conflict-atop-Money so close to the question stone and to Comfort, Negativity, and Change, it was my feeling that their financial woes were existent long before any surgery. Stress, tension, and even shouting matches and quarrels were indicated. A divorce or separation seemed at hand, or at least some kind of change that could then lead to Beneficial Gain. To my way of thinking, this situation was hurting her more than her husband (notice the dagger's point and remember her low self-esteem). If any split occurred, it would probably be when she could no longer cope with the situation.

RESPONSE AND RESULTS

The woman's surprised face was soon awash in tears. "No truer words have ever been spoken," she sobbed. This latest surgery had indeed been the "last straw," bringing to light three years of money mismanagement, even though she and her husband each had good jobs. The disinterest and withdrawal of her husband had also become apparent. She claimed that he insisted he didn't know how to relate to her or understand what she expected of him (notice the alignment of Man and Confusion far away from Woman). When I asked more questions, I learned that the idea of marriage had been his, not hers, but that she had gone along with it so as not to lose him. The love between them was real enough, but neither could stand the other's personality traits or personal habits. They were destroying each other, yet neither wanted to alter his or her own long-standing behavior patterns. Her list of grievances was so excessive that I skirted the subject altogether, and made the following recommendations: "Since you are incapable right now of fending for yourself, and he is making no demands of you, call a truce. Give the situation another chance, and give yourself time to heal. Be pleasant and forgiving and bide your time. It sounds to me as if you're trying too hard and expecting too much. This is an old problem, not a new one, and it will not be solved overnight. The strain you've been under lately and the pain you've been suffering have intensified the differences you've had with your husband since you first met. I sense that neither of you knows how to communicate with the other effectively or how to listen nonjudgmentally. If you want the freedom to make a new choice, you must also grant that same privilege to him, unconditionally. When you feel better, pursue marriage counseling and/or classes in the true art of communication and in how to build a positive self-image."

A year and half later, I received a letter from the woman. Her husband had refused marriage counseling and classes, so she had gone ahead without him and done both. She had grown tremendously from the experience, while he had stagnated. This had resulted in divorce. She had then quit her job, rented a U-Haul, and moved bag and baggage to another state for a complete environment change. A photograph enclosed with the letter showed her to be slimmer, healthier-looking, and exuding a happy self-confidence. The divorce shook up the husband so much that he was apparently forced to reassess his behavior and go to a counselor. Both people gained from what had once been an unfortunate mismatch.

Sample M

In our current economic situation, with so many people being laid off work nationwide, money questions now outrank those about love. The following came from two sisters (one was the spokesperson): "My sister and I are thinking of going into business together, a creative business. Will we be successful?"

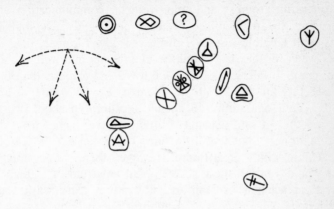

THE CAST

The question stone is female; my eyes radiated out as shown. A surge of joy filled me when I looked at this cast. Notice Beneficial Gain and Money fairly close to the question stone on one side and the Fire glyph on the other, with Man somewhat removed (as if the men in their lives were supportive but not directly involved). Then notice the lineup below the question stone of Woman, Love, Marriage, and Gifts. A move is close at hand, with Change and Home to the right of the lineup. Negativity seems a thing of the past, yet take note of Comfort and Conflict. They seem to convey a warning with their detached position at the bottom-left side of the lineup. Confusion skipped away from the cast, so I returned it to the pouch.

INTERPRETATION

"Yes" was the obvious answer, "as long as you always remember to stay on top of your market and keep up with trends. Educate, communicate, advertise, be actively engaged in customer outreach. Know the people you seek to target, plus their desires and needs." I based this comment on the strong

positioning of Beneficial Gain between the question stone and
Money, with Fire to the right (signifying the unusual "rightness"
of this venture). Keep in mind that the Beneficial Gain rune
also concerns progress and improvement, communication and
advertising, the marketplace of ideas and trends, accomplishments with tangible results. I discussed how fortunate the two
sisters were, for they truly could work together and well, a good
combination of talent in which each loves and respects the other
(include Fire in the lineup of Woman, Love, Marriage, and
Gifts). "Your operation will change locations in about two to
three months," I said (Change a little over two inches from the
question stone), "but you'll do fine. This is an excellent business venture with a great future. However, there is one glitch."
What would you tell these sisters about any kind of "glitch"?
Study the placement of Comfort and Conflict. Mine was a one-
word reply: "*Complacency.*" I advised that everything was so
good about their business plans that it was almost too good.
Thus, they would probably have a tendency to lay back or delay
or disregard what really needed attention, including any personal disagreements that should have a hearing. "It may be
a question of comfort versus work schedules, success versus
continuous efforting. Complacency may blind you to the very
issues which could make or break your business."

RESPONSE AND RESULTS

An animated and enthusiastic dialogue followed, in which the
sisters revealed that their business idea was the making of hand-
bags. And yes, they would be moving their work location in
about two months, since demand for their clever renditions was
already exceeding what they could produce where they were.
They took my warning to heart, and the last I heard, their
business was booming . . . a testament to the relevancy of the
entrepreneurial spirit.

Sample N

I will conclude the samples in this section with two that deal
with issues of a controversial nature for women. Sample N

covers the ramifications of ending a pregnancy, and was asked by a slender, middle-aged woman who had been married for some time. "What are the spiritual and moral implications of abortion?"

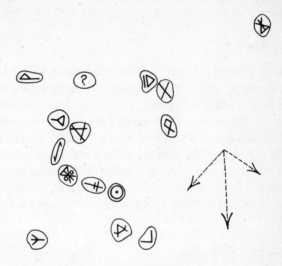

THE CAST

Nonpersonal and/or political questions are fascinating to address through the casting process, but this cast, as with Sample L, did not match the question asked. It was obvious to me that the woman was being evasive. Study this cast carefully. The question stone is female and my eyes radiated out as shown. Since Change sometimes refers to death, doesn't it look as if this woman had just lost or aborted a female baby? Notice Comfort, isolated to the left of the question stone, suggesting that the whole issue of abortion was either being treated flippantly here or somehow being downplayed. Then trace Home, Gifts, and Beneficial Gain, equally isolated but to the right, highlighting a prosperous life with all the amenities. Now move straight down from the question stone to the curving lineup of Woman, Confusion, Change, Marriage, Negativity, Money (signaling that pregnancies in this family might be of a lesser priority than career advancement); also include Conflict and Fire, which indicate a deep-seated spiritual conflict. Man (her husband) is removed to the lower left, as if he were disinterested. Love is high to the right, appearing to me as if the soul of the female baby were still around and seeking expression.

INTERPRETATION

I chose to disregard what seemed pretentious to me and went right to the heart of the *real* question: "You just aborted a little girl and you're filled with guilt, aren't you?" The woman bolted up from her chair, her mouth flung open as if to scream at me, when she suddenly stopped short, stiffened, glared out into space for what seemed minutes, then lost herself in a flood of tears as her body collapsed in a heap. Without saying a word, she conveyed all that needed to be said. Gently, I touched her arm and said, "I'm here for you. If you want, we can talk about this." She nodded in the affirmative.

RESPONSE AND RESULTS

Her story gave me pause. She had married after a few years of college, with no clear sense of what her future might be or what she wanted out of life. She and her husband were happy enough, and they discussed everything together before reaching a decision. Yet whatever they decided upon always reflected their intellect, not their heart. A balanced viewpoint, giving each aspect of their lives (physical, mental, emotional, and spiritual) equal weight, never seemed to happen. They had three sons, which pleased her husband, but the "price" she had paid for those boys was dear. She had had four abortions and two miscarriages. Each of the aborted babies had been female (gender was known only after the fact). She did not mention the sex of those she had miscarried. Her husband was at peace over the whole thing, but she was holding out for another pregnancy. "Did you ever tell your husband how you really feel about the abortions, especially the fact that they were all female?" I queried. "No," she whispered. "It doesn't seem to matter to him."

The grief of her guilt was manifesting in the form of depression, mood swings, loss of appetite, complete loss of self-esteem, plus a host of physical ailments. She was under a doctor's care, but she had admitted to no one the true extent of her problem or the great sense of loss she was feeling. I recommended professional counseling—for both of them!—and I also urged her to seek out a grief counselor, someone whose specialty is death and its many ramifications, including that of fetal death.

Then I suggested the following: "In a relaxed state of meditation, contact the soul of the child you have aborted and invite her to speak to you. Open yourself to whatever pops into your mind. Do not judge what ensues. Let happen what happens. Give the third party in this situation a chance to be heard. I think you will find that she can help you to discover what the *female within you,* your deepest self, wants." At my insistence, the woman agreed to tell her husband what she had told me and then to get the help she needed before considering any more pregnancies. This case is typical of the quandary faced by many women today. That's because the issue of abortion covers more than just physical processes versus the right of choice. It also addresses the deeper needs of *both* women and men, *plus* that of the soul seeking entry. Parental education and counseling make a tremendous difference, along with a supportive environment for whatever choice is made; but what about the soul of the third party? Wisdom suggests that some attempt at soul contact be made—perhaps through meditation, prayer, dreams, or even psychic means—to see what is truly best for the highest good of *all* concerned, not just for the mother or the father.

Sample O

The last of these samples addresses the subject of personal power, although that is not how the question was asked. A single woman, feeling overwhelmed by a great sense of fear and abandonment, wanted to know: "How do I get in touch with my heart?"

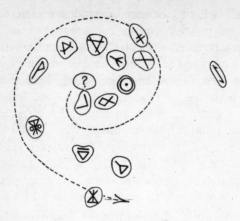

THE CAST

I already knew the situation this woman was in, even though I had never met or spoken with her one-on-one. Hers was the spiritual quest, and her commitment had been to join forces with a charismatic leader of a spiritual community, a man who had suddenly died. She was left in charge of winding up many of his affairs. My vision spiraled counterclockwise around the female question stone, and in doing so, I came to realize this question had more to do with power issues than with those of the heart (Love is the last rune in the lineup of glyphs that curve around the question stone). Fire abuts the question stone, setting the theme for the entire cast—the consuming power of spirit. Also affirmed by this positioning is the rightness of her present situation for her continued growth. The curving lineup of glyphs after Fire shows me that she is a gifted communicator/ writer/teacher (Beneficial Gain), perfectly capable of making a good living on her own, and was probably involved in the community finances (Money), that she was strongly attracted to the leader and deferred to him (Man with the extra glyphs of Gifts and Negativity close by—note that Negativity points *away* from her), and that she probably feels more than just abandonment because the man died (Man followed by Confusion, Conflict, Comfort). Marriage, Home, Woman, and Love, toward the end of the lineup, tell me that she is headed for more social and work relationships with women and, because of this, will come to reevaluate her worth as a female in a very positive way.

INTERPRETATION

"You gave your power away to this man and you're afraid to admit how angry you are that he died on you, leaving you stripped bare of the security you thought you had." Her sad face perked up. "Your question is not about reclaiming your heart energies. It's about personal power—recognizing, respecting, and expressing your own worth as an equally valuable participant in this school we call the earthplane." This statement got her full attention. I encouraged her to face her anger, to take a long, hard look at her situation: why she had joined the community, the many years she had devoted to the leader and his vision (forgetting herself and her own needs in the process), how she really felt about his choice not to prolong his life, and the way his followers had fled the community during the final hours—like "rats fleeing a sinking ship." "What happened at the community is a reflection of how you abandoned yourself when you first joined. Certainly, community-based living can be a very positive and enriching experience, one that teaches respect and cooperation and responsible caring and sharing. But when you joined, you gave away any personal identification with the self of your being, literally denying the wonder of your own creativity and intelligence. That wasn't necessary."

RESPONSE AND RESULTS

There was some dialogue between us, but I could see that she was finding our session rather overwhelming and difficult to take. Thus, I backed off from any more comments about the community, and instead invited her to gaze at the cast in a detached manner. "What does its shape remind you of?" I asked. "A seashell, like a nautilus," she replied. I seized on this to say that she will come out of this situation, unfolding the magic of her being from the core of the nautilus shell, through all the walled-in compartments she had thought she was trapped in, unfurling as if a flag toward the broad, open doorway that awaited her. "There is a new organization or business involvement ahead of you, one which involves women or is headed by a woman, where you can develop yourself and feel good about yourself as never before. Your spiritual quest is still a valid one, but only if you honor the uniqueness of your own life gifts. You will find your heart when you claim the power you are."

Six months later, the woman telephoned. She was effusive in her praise for the rune casting, saying it helped her face what she did not want to see. Although she was still affiliated with the community, there had been many changes, not least of which was female management. Without leaving the property, she was literally working for a new organization, one that had recognized her talent, promoted her, and given her responsible assignments. She sounded confident, enthusiastic, and very much wiser for her ordeal. Her case reminded me of how easily feminine energy can be miscast, especially under the guise of "spiritual guidance" and male power issues. It seems to me that spirit speaks more readily through people who accept the divinity in themselves and others than it does through the "divine" rantings or overbloated egos of any single individual, male *or* female.

These samples should give you an idea of the process of rune casting, and of the importance of honoring your feelings when a given question is asked. Please do not allow yourself to be limited by my interpretations, but rather, use them as a springboard for developing your own personal methods and style. What works for you is what counts, not what works for me. Do not feel you are "wrong" if your methods differ from mine. Experiment. Play. Demonstrate. Test yourself and the runes you use. You can determine what works for you only by hands-on experience. Runes do not work from your head—they extend from your heart.

I am partial to the art of casting because it is uninhibited and free of restraints while still offering a reliable "lens" through which infinite patterns of light and darkness, mind and spirit, can be viewed. Rune casting depends on "flow" and a trust in one's own intuition. There are no formats and no limitations other than those you invent for yourself.

Regardless of how you may use runes, they will faithfully lead you through the depths of the inner self to the primordial magic of sacredness. They will enable you to become a child again—in a world that tolerates only adults.

Runes have a strange way of highlighting the subconscious *objectively* and the conscious *subjectively,* which is exactly backward. This can be disconcerting until you get used to it. But then, this is why rune casting is so much fun ... it is completely unpredictable.

CHAPTER FIVE

Past-Life Samples to Consider

Rune casting, as a type of "spiritual calisthenics," can help you to realign your thought processes. The way it stimulates synergy between left- and right-brain hemispheres tends to promote whole brain development. But that's not all. You can deepen the experience even further. The Way of A Cast can become the way to step beyond present-life activities to possible past-life memories. The intuitive leap that you make when using Goddess Runes in this manner can plunge you into the core dynamics of your very beginnings, revealing, as it does, the story lines of lives unnumbered.

Although past-life information may seem nebulous at best, little more than an excursion into the heart of fantasy and wish fulfillment, I have seen amazing healings come about when people choose to face whatever might exist within their deepest selves. And invariably, such a choice leads them to acknowledge that something quite real and valid undergirds the concept of reincarnation.

In the middle sixties, when I began a practice in hypnotic past-life regressions, I insisted on obtaining the type of data from my hypnotized clients that would be checked historically. Sometimes I was successful; most times I wasn't. Years later, two unusual cases came my way. The healings that resulted from these sessions defied logic or reason. Experiencing this, seeing firsthand what happened to the people involved, changed not only my practice—it changed me. From that moment on, I cared nary a whit for any type of "proof." Instead, I sought only to assist my clients in accessing whatever memories or sources of information would be helpful for them to better understand their current life situations and live in a more positive and constructive manner. My practice suddenly skyrocketed when I did this, and healings increased substantially. When I "retired" to pursue my own spiritual journey, I felt blessed beyond measure to have had the privilege of sharing in the intimate awakenings of so many individuals.

Decades later, a man queried of the runes, "Tell me about my past lives." Much to my surprise, the cast complied. After thousands of such castings, I have learned that hypnosis isn't necessary; you really can obtain past-life information quickly and easily with Goddess Runes. Anyone can do it.

It was Christian D. Larson, a gifted mystic in the late 1800s, who is quoted as saying: "We cannot know the truth by what seems to be true from a single point of view." Rune casting addresses this insightful comment by providing yet another way to broaden our perspective. Since The Way of A Cast is unlimited, the sources one can contact are equally so.

Casting for past-life material is done basically in the same manner as what you have already learned. I've noticed a few differences, though, and would like to share them with you:

• Consult your own intuition first to determine if it is appropriate for you to proceed. This can be done either during the ritual you employ at the start of your session (a good method for beginners) or during any moment when you are able to relax, center yourself, and ask your inner source what is the proper action to take (a good method for the more experienced).

• If it feels right to continue, and to engage in casting, ask the querist if there is any particular goal he or she wants to accomplish during the session (clarify intent, even if you are casting for yourself). If none is declared, seek for whichever past life directly affects the present one, affirming in your mind that only information for the highest good of all concerned can come forth.

• Observe a few moments of silence after you have cast. Gaze at the runes loosely, without paying much attention to what is there, and devoid of any particular thought.

• Now, within the quiet of your mind, ask yourself each of the questions listed below, hesitating after each one so an answer can be revealed or somehow make itself known:

  1. Is this a previous lifetime I see before me?

  2. Is the individual male or female in this previous life?

  3. Am I privy to the entire spread of this lifetime, or to only a part of it?

  4. Where does this life take place? In more than one major area or country?

  5. About what time in history is covered here?

  6. How do I begin to interpret what I see before me?

These six questions set the stage for you as a rune caster. You now have all the information needed to enable you to relax into the cast and to advance through the lifetime in front of you, saying out loud what you see and sense as you go along. Do not hesitate once you begin.

When I do this particular type of casting I request that no one interrupt me until I am finished because I tend to function as a conscious "channel" in the way information flows. The more I surrender to the moment, knowing full well that I am protected and guided, the more details surface in my mind. Many people, like me, can enter into such a cast so deeply that the lifetime revealed becomes alive with sights, sounds, smells, and feelings. If you are not able to reach this depth, you can still use each runic glyph as a signal or flag to help you arrange tidbits of information in a way that seems to convey a story line. Even scanty renderings can be "earthshaking" if what you are saying resonates with the questioner. It is not necessary for you to understand the material you receive. It is only necessary that you retain the clarity of your connection with the source you have contacted. You can dialogue with your questioner later.

I want to make it clear that when casting for past-life material, the details of a past-life story do not necessarily come bursting forth in one great sweep of inspiration. They can, but seldom is that the case. Usually the initial direction you need impresses itself on your consciousness at the onset, and then details surface as you go along. The more you talk, the more the story line begins to unfold, inspiring the questioner as well. Tap into past-life memories, and the resulting session can become electric in the way snatches of this and that, childhood dreams, promptings that made no sense before, and unusual feelings all seem to come together and make so much sense that it is almost as if some hidden obstacle were removed and a deeper truth freed.

If you are doing past-life castings for yourself, be certain to make a drawing of the cast, then record on paper or with a tape recorder what your initial feelings and reactions are, any information that comes to mind. Put your drawing away for about a week. During that time, in prayer or however you contact The Source of Your Being for guidance, ask for further clarification of the cast—perhaps when you are dreaming at night, or when you meditate. Do not make the mistake of accepting your first impressions as "the way it is." Give yourself ample time to distance yourself from any story that emerged, so you can better ensure the kind of objectivity and discernment that are possible through detachment. At week's end, read or play back your recording of the interpretation you originally felt prompted to give, comparing it with any information that might have surfaced since. I think you will be amazed at what results, and the meaning it will have for you.

Casting for information about your own past-life sojourns is like stepping into your dreams in search of the *real* dreamer and discovering to your joy the glorious reality of "soul."

Whether true in the literal sense or not, these "memories" help you to uncover layers of the psyche in a quest for understanding and wholeness. They help you to heal whatever is unbalanced, misdirected, or underdeveloped. Keep this in mind when you do past-life castings for other people, as you may need to counsel the individual afterward about the importance of learning from previous misjudgments . . . and of forgiveness.

Albert Einstein once said, "Time and space are modes by which we think, not conditions in which we live." You will find this to be true if you explore the concept of reincarnation and what it implies.

As in Chapter Four, I have prepared a number of actual casts so you can see how I work. Study the samples one at a time, asking yourself how *you* would interpret it before you read how the cast stimulated the intuitive wellspring within me. Obviously, past-life casting relies heavily on guidance from levels that extend past the "norm." It represents an advancement in rune use, plus a way to develop even greater sensitivity and psychic awareness in your own life. As regular casting is a brain changer, past-life casting is *a brain stretcher*.

The more you do it, the better you become. The key here is attitude. Make yours one of joy. Regardless of how real or unreal reincarnational memories are, the effect they have on people, the incredible changes that can result from accessing them, make past-life casting an invaluable tool for personal growth and transformation.

Sample A

Many people prefer to explore the possibility of past lives through telephone sessions. I suspect the privacy and convenience of remaining in their own home appeals to them. This was one such event, when two young women, each on a separate extension, asked this question (all the while giggling and laughing): "Were we ever in a past life together, maybe as sisters?"

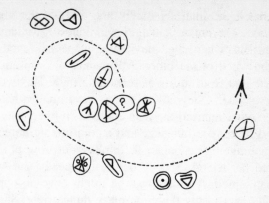

THE CAST

In the silence of my own spiritual center that I perceive at the core of my being, I suddenly became intuitively aware of a previous existence for these two women, not as sisters, but as girlfriends. My sense was that this took place in the Roaring Twenties in the United States, and that only sections of that life were pictured here. With that initial impression to set the stage, I gazed at the casting and soon found myself focusing on what appeared to be a love triangle (notice Man and Love on either side of Confusion, which is atop the female question stone), and on that seemed like a tremendous conflict between the two women over this situation (Negativity pointed at Conflict as an extension of the love triangle). My eye movement wound in a counterclockwise spiral, highlighting as it did a schism that developed (Change so close to Conflict). One woman left on her own (Woman, Beneficial Gain), while the other stayed to marry the man (Fire followed by Marriage, Comfort, Money, Home). Gifts at the end of the cast impressed me as a wish left unfulfilled at life's end.

INTERPRETATION

The story I relayed concerned two female friends who happened to have fallen in love with the same man. They had each

met and dated the man separately and without the knowledge
of the other. The entire situation was innocent of any malice
or deceit. But when the inevitable happened, each woman
thought the worst of the other. All manner of accusations were
hurled back and forth in fits of screaming rage. The two women
parted in a huff. One moved away, never to be heard from
again. The other married the man and had children. She enjoyed
a long and successful marriage and a comfortable home. As the
married one aged, she began to think about how unfairly she
had treated her friend. Shortly before her death, she wished in
prayer that someday, somehow, she might have an opportunity
to do it all again—only this time make things right. She wanted
to heal the fractured relationship with her former girlfriend.

RESPONSE AND RESULTS

The two women on the phone were beside themselves. One
spoke up immediately: "And we did it again, twice. Can you
imagine that? Twice. And each time I was at her throat, accus-
ing her of everything imaginable." The other broke in. "I
wasn't guilty, ever! She believed what other people told her.
She never asked me anything." As the details of their story
tumbled forth, one told of finally garnering enough courage to
meet with her friend and talk out their differences. Revelation
after revelation resulted. After the meeting, they emerged the
best of friends. Apparently both of them had consistently mis-
judged each other, and had depended on the opinions of other
people instead of seeking the truth for themselves. Boyfriends
had been lost, feelings hurt. "I hope you two realize what has
happened here," I interjected. "That meeting you had wasn't
just two women talking things out. It was an opportunity for
the two of you to heal at the soul level and correct a wrongful
action done long ago. In healing that, you have opened the way
for both of you to achieve even greater happiness and joy in
this life. I congratulate you for what you have done!" Yes, the
one who had initiated that fateful meeting in this life was the

married woman who had made the wish "the last time around." Her wish came true.

Sample B

A woman in her early thirties came to me and asked this simple question: "Which of my past lives is having the most effect on my life now?"

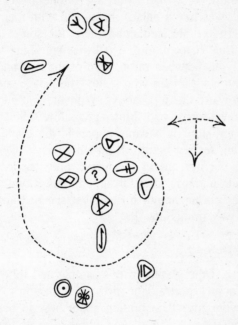

THE CAST

During the period of silence, I began to focus on a female lifetime in what would now be called Lebanon, although then it seemed to be part of Assyria. My intuitive sense was that I was being shown a full life spread that took place before the coming of the man Jesus. Negativity pointing through the female question stone at Beneficial Gain made it clear to me that girls were not educated at this time in history, and for her this was especially painful. Her youth was spent in a religious home

(Fire close to the question stone), yet she was allowed to develop her talent for dance (Woman and Gifts together as they are here impressed me as signifying a feminine talent acceptable to society then, hence dance). Because of her inability to accept the dictums of her family (Confusion beneath the question stone), she was sent away to another city (Change followed by Home) to become something akin to a governess for the children of a wealthy landowner (Marriage, Money). My sense was that this place was like a palace, busy, and with many servants and much activity. She remained there for some time (with either a radiating vision line or clockwise spiraling, there is an absence of glyphs between the bottom of the cast and the top). She fell in love with a man who visited the palace and left with him (Love toward the top, above Woman, and in a natural sequence from Money and Marriage below). She was very happy with him until it became apparent she could not have sons. The Man, feeling betrayed, turned abusive (Conflict) and beat her, kicking her out of his home. She wandered around the countryside until she died of her injuries. Comfort showed me that there was no hatred in her, that she had accepted her fate as "the way things are."

INTERPRETATION

Just looking at the glyphs in this sample and following both vision lines amply portray the flow of a person's life. Once you receive your initial inspiration about how to begin, either information just "pops" into your mind or your feelings will somehow lead you along until you begin to make connections. Confusion and doubt arise only when you distrust the process.

RESPONSE AND RESULTS

My questioner interrupted the brief musings I offered and took charge of the session. Visibly shaken, she spoke of having been overpowered since childhood by an urge to marry young and have sons. She did, bringing forth two. She expressed the strong feeling that the man she had married was the same one as in the cast. Once again, he had become abusive and had beaten her. This time, however, she had garnered enough courage to stand her ground and obtain a divorce. A reader all her life, she admitted to dancing for her own amusement whenever her nose was not in a book. Dissatisfied with structured religion, she had embarked upon her own spiritual quest, discovering as she did the power of meditation and prayer. She further described the classes she was taking toward earning a college degree. Then she added, "Wealthy people do not hold me in awe. The way they live seems natural to me, familiar."

If ever there was an example of how a cast can inspire a questioner to do his or her own interpretation, it is this one. Once I had verbalized my initial sense of what I saw pictured before me, the woman intervened. She made her own connections and supplied her own meanings. The more she talked, the more involved she became—until, I swear, the years rolled back and she was able to reclaim the youthful beauty she had once been. How could one possibly care whether or not this woman had ever lived a previous life in ancient Assyria? What matters to me is that this incredible story resonated as true *for her* and she was transformed *by the power of telling it*.

Sample C

A concerned mother came to me one day and moaned: "I am worried about my young daughter. Is there a past life of hers that is affecting her present one?"

THE CAST

The question stone is female; my eyes radiated as shown. Immediately the state of Kentucky popped into my mind and, in the silence, I connected with the time of the Great Depression. As I began to view the runic glyphs, my eyes affixed to the tight lineup near the question stone where Negativity pointed at Man and Conflict. Obviously, there was trouble in this home. But I was stuck there, and none of the other glyphs made any sense until I realized that I should have spiraled instead of radi-

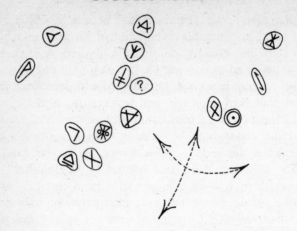

ated. Either in your mind or directly on this book page, trace a counterclockwise spiral from Negativity over to Woman and Comfort, then down to the cluster of glyphs below the question stone (Fire, Home, Gifts, Marriage, Confusion) and continuing on to Beneficial Gain, Money, Change, and Love at the far right. When I did this, the "puzzle pieces" fell into place and the cast made sense to me. This was a female who had been badly abused by her father (the lineup near the question stone), removed from the situation (Woman, Comfort), adopted out (the cluster below the question stone), educated (Beneficial Gain), employed (Money), and had moved away (Change) and found the love of her life (Love). Obviously, an entire life was pictured here.

INTERPRETATION

The story I was compelled to tell had a sad beginning. Distressed and chronically unemployed, the girl's father had turned to alcohol. In a fit of rage, he had beaten and abused his wife and two sons, and raped his four-year-old daughter. He was imprisoned for life. The mother's beatings left her unable to care for her children, so each was adopted out to different families. The young daughter was relieved to go, finding life as a ward of the state preferable to what she had endured at home.

The people who later adopted her were good and caring people, religious, with a boy and a girl of their own. Theirs was a happy and active household, yet she remained ever the loner— a child apart—confused by memories that were disturbing to her. She graduated from high school and vocational training, becoming a secretary, until the day came when she was offered a proposal of marriage from a man who lived in another state. She accepted his offer and moved, finding him to be the love of her life after she arrived. My sense was she could not have children because of what her father had done to her, but her life with her husband was enjoyable nonetheless.

RESPONSE AND RESULTS

The woman's mouth dropped open in amazement. "My God," she exclaimed, "she was sexually abused in this life, too. She was only eighteen months old when a female baby-sitter I had hired tortured her sexually. By the time I discovered what had happened, the baby-sitter had skipped town. The police are still looking for the woman. And her father deserted us. There are so many unresolved issues around him. My daughter is now four, and she is so angry it is difficult for me to handle her." Sensing the repeat of a previous tragedy, I looked the mother straight in the eye and in a firm voice said, "Immediately, today is not too soon, find a good psychologist for both you and your daughter and make an appointment. You may or may not choose to tell the psychologist about this casting, but do tell him or her about what has been happening in this present lifetime. You both need professional help *right now,* and I suspect you also need some advice about how to resolve any lingering problems concerning the child's father."

One of the things I've noticed when seeking to uncover reincarnational memories is that unresolved issues from any previous sojourn *or* deeply engrained habit patterns *will repeat from life to life* until that individual soul recognizes what is happening and chooses to change things, beginning with the attitudes and actions of the "self."

Recently I did a series of castings for a young man who, since childhood, had been compulsively drawn to any material he could find about John F. Kennedy's assassination and the Holocaust in Nazi Germany during World War II. Yes, he did seem to have been alive during both of these time frames, but not living the kind of life I would have assumed (*never allow personal opinions to enter your mind when casting;* flow with impressions as they are received). During each period, my intuitive sense placed him as the devoted son of wealthy parents who behaved in accordance with his parents' wishes—until confronted with bigotry and injustice. In the German life, he fled the country after seeing what was happening to Jews, joined the Resistance movement, and died in an explosion. Without much of a "layover," he promptly reincarnated, this time in Alabama, reaching his teen years during the Freedom March. His refusal to support the fundamentalist beliefs of his religious parents was short-lived. He acquiesced under heavy pressure from them, later dying of pneumonia after severe bouts with depression. In both cases, bigotry and injustice became focal points for a confrontation with parental authority. He declared the validity and value of his own perceptions in the German life, but in the Southern one, he sank into a morass of guilt—not about what was happening to blacks, but about his own failure to stand up for himself. When I queried his current status, he replied, "Well, I did it again. I'm the devoted son of wealthy Boston Catholics, and I have a decision to make. I cannot live the way my parents want me to, yet if I buck them I'll lose my inheritance." I don't know what the young man finally decided, but I do know that he had a lot to think about after those castings. His case further illustrates that the soul will keep repeating lessons, even altering how they are "played" out, until whatever needs to be learned *is learned.*

Sample D

A happily married woman and mother of four wondered: "What past life would be the most beneficial for me to look at now?"

THE CAST

In the silence of my center, I perceived that this woman had experienced a lifetime as a female in the ancient homeland of Macedonia, located on the Balkan Peninsula. My intuitive sense was that a whole story line lay before me, one that would have a surprising effect on my questioner once it was explored. Love close to the question stone told me that her childhood had been a good one. Following Love is Home (she entered another environment), Fire (probably a religious order), and Woman (mostly female members). With my eye movement radiating to the left, I noticed a cluster of glyphs (Man, Confusion, Marriage, Negativity, and Comfort) that showed me that she stayed away from men and refused marriage. When I gazed straight down, Money signaled to me that this woman never wanted for anything and was well provided for, until a tragedy of major proportions struck (Change, Conflict, Gifts). Her role then altered to that of a communicator or networker (Beneficial Gain).

INTERPRETATION

The more I relaxed into this cast, the more clearly focused the lifetime became. Suddenly, as if I were witnessing a Hollywood movie, the whole scenario revealed itself. Here is what I saw: she was a beautiful child, a beloved treasure who was dedicated to "temple" work at an early age. Her many talents centered around an exceptional understanding of music and a higher purpose for dance. Her regimen at the religious order allowed her to experiment with the other female members with various types of sound and movement, and then with the public at large. Since her parents were wealthy, she was afforded extra privileges that she used to further her study of tonal rhythms and their healing power. She refused all offers of marriage, feeling that such unions were much too political and one-sided for her tastes. Her dedication to her work became a lifetime commitment. Then a major earthquake hit. The devastation was so severe, the very culture of her country was threatened. Without a second thought, she left the order and assumed a leadership role in helping to rebuild. Functioning as a "city planner," she closely monitored relief efforts and reconstruction. She never once looked back or had any regrets about her choice to put her country first. She died of exhaustion.

RESPONSE AND RESULTS

If I would have had a camera, I could have snapped a photo of the woman's face as proof of how the story I told affected her. Her mouth fell open, her eyes brightened, and her face glowed rosy pink. She could hardly talk, she was so excited. "My grandparents live in Croatia. My parents are emigrants from Yugoslavia. When I learned how to walk, I was taught all the folk dances of the Balkan countries, with special emphasis on the history of Macedonia." As if this revelation weren't surprising enough, she went on to admit that she lacked self-confidence in making her own decisions. Her children were now in high school, she and her husband were financially secure, yet she agonized about informing her family that she wanted to learn how to make stained-glass windows in the hope of setting up her own studio. She also wanted to travel by herself on occasion and engage in research on various ways to use art as therapy for healing. Her frustration with her inability to express her needs and desires had resulted in embarrassing and irrational mood swings. I invited her to get acquainted with the powerful personality she had once had, perhaps through dreams or in meditation, and just *feel* what it is like to be self-directed. Through various exercises in imagery and role-playing, she was able to loosen up and feel better about herself. "You do not want to re-create who you were in the past," I cautioned. "But it is appropriate to reach back on occasion and bring forward those positive qualities which could enhance the life you have now." The lady did just that, much to the delight of her husband and children. Her mood swings vanished.

Sample E

Here follow three castings, all done for the same woman, who was searching for a sense of purpose and meaning after the untimely death of her husband the previous year from leukemia. "I would like to know about past-life connections between me and my husband."

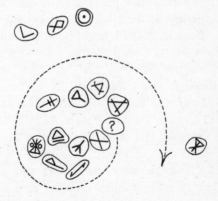

THE CAST

This first cast concentrates on a tight cluster, literally a circle within a circle, illustrating for me the intrigue of a close family unit with "secrets" (Gifts, Man, Home, Marriage, Comfort, Change, overshadowed by Confusion, Conflict, Woman, Negativity). A female question stone is used, and my eye movement spirals clockwise. My mind locked into a time around 1910 in Albany, New York, or perhaps in Massachusetts. The son in this family I sensed was in actuality my female questioner; the mother, my questioner's husband (note the gender reversals).

INTERPRETATION

This full spread portrays a fascinating tale. I intuitively felt it was a traditional home—Mom, Dad, and two children, a boy and a girl. The girl died of a fever, leaving the son as an "only child." Family life was happy, with each member devoted to the others. The son was extremely curious, a reader par excellence, who achieved a college degree. His father died shortly after his graduation, so he moved back home and remained there, as a companion to his mother, while employed nearby. It didn't take long before he noticed that his mother had strange mood swings and deep depressions, sometimes lapsing into paranoia and schizophrenic-type symptoms. He hired a female nurse to care for her at their home, and helped whenever he could. Money, Beneficial Gain, and Fire (overlooking the cast) led me to believe he was employed as a seminary college professor, specializing in theology and law. Any extracurricular activities he shunned, any opportunity for romance he avoided (no other glyphs in the outer perimeter/upper section), as he felt duty-bound to care for his mother—which he did until it was no longer feasible. Her rages increased to the point that he finally had to have her committed to a mental hospital, where she went totally mad. He later fell in love and married (Love lower right), but refused to father children as a way to ensure that his mother's insanity could not be inherited. He had known all along that his mother had always been "strange," a dark secret the father did not know himself until his wife's father finally confessed the truth. My sense is that the son's childhood dreams are the reason he knew more than his father did.

"Where did the strong bond between son and mother come from? What led up to this?" asked my questioner.

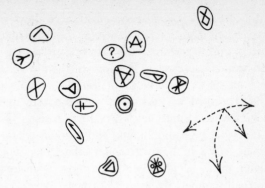

THE CAST

The question stone is female; my eyes radiated as shown. I could not get a fix on any particular country, except a feeling for Europe, perhaps in the early 1800s. I saw a time period beset by war and regional conflicts (notice Conflict and Confusion closest to the question stone, then include Comfort and Love nearby and Negativity pointed at Money). My intuitive sense was that the son was now a brother, and the mother from the last cast was now the sister in a family under attack (the positioning of Conflict). The Beneficial Gain rune in the far right (apart from the others) alerted me to a unique form of communication between the two siblings (also include Fire and Gifts, as this is often a sign of psychic ability). The sister was the most affected by the war (Woman close to Negativity). The two escaped and roamed far and wide until their deaths (Change, Home, Marriage).

INTERPRETATION

The war I "witnessed" in my inner eye was vicious. Atrocities were committed on all sides. The two siblings managed to survive, although their parents and several other brothers and sisters were killed. They lived because of the uncanny ability each possessed to psychically "tune in" to each other. The sister was exposed to more horror than the brother, plus she was sexually attacked several times. Although the brother was able to rescue her in the "nick of time," she became fearful, skittish, easily upset, and anxious. She relaxed and was happy only in her brother's presence. Because of their psychic ability, they were both quite resourceful in finding suitable places to live. Neither received an education, nor did they have much money—which was a continual worry for the sister. They traveled over land and high mountains, and worked whenever they could; she died of a high fever, water-relatedlike typhoid, and he years later in an accident while he was repairing a house. During their subsequent life in the Northeast, when the brother was the son and the sister was the mother, he "remembered" the war and all that had happened (that memory returning to him in the dream state). This is why he was always patient and kind while caring for his ailing mother. *He knew that the real cause of her insanity was what had happened to her in their previous existence.* He watched over her this second time as he had once done when he was her brother in Europe, repeating his guardianship role, without the slightest hesitation as to what might become of him.

For the third cast, my questioner asked: "What is the meaning of our present life together?"

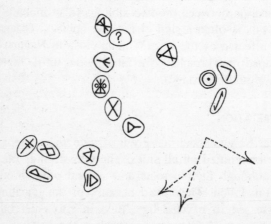

THE CAST

Love—elevated and next to the female question stone—is the theme of this cast. Notice the horseshoe shape that involves Woman, Gifts, Marriage, Man, Love, the question stone, Confusion, Money, Fire, and Change. Pay attention to separate activity at the lower left, with Negativity, Beneficial Gain, Conflict, Home, and Comfort forming a circle. Study this casting. With what you already know about these two souls, how would you answer the questioner?

INTERPRETATION

My answer was simple: the grace of true love. To me, theirs was a most exquisite and special love story, a story of sacrifice and caring, of one soul shelving all other plans to aid and help another who was in distress. I suspected that the husband had developed health problems early in the marriage: blood-count deviations, slurred speech, lack of control of body functions. This was embarrassing to him and very uncomfortable. He would have spent much time in the hospital, and in being ill. This, I felt, angered him. The pain would have been tremendous. "Yet you were there for him," I noted, "ever at his side, with no complaints and no regrets, even though the situation was difficult for you. When he died, you were left richer for what happened, probably financially as per insurance claims, but more importantly because of the confidence and peace you gained from the 'rich' interactions and sharing the two of you had. In my opinion, his death was grace and his illness a gift. The nightmare of that war two lifetimes ago was expunged in this life thanks to the 'cleansing fire' of leukemia. Because you chose to stay, no matter how long it might take, to help this soul work through the pain of the past, I am certain you have both gained spiritually and you are both free."

RESPONSE AND RESULTS

My questioner drew close to me and shared how much sense the castings made to her, and how accurate I was about what happened to her husband after they were married. "Paul faced his circumstances very bravely. I was talking with his sister about this during the holidays. She told me that ever since childhood, facing life with *courage* had always been very important to Paul. The bond between us that you mentioned was a trademark of our relationship. I did not fall in love with him at first sight, but I fell in 'like' with him the moment I met him. It does not upset me in the least when you say that there was a purpose to all the suffering. It just plain adds up!"

Sometimes the roots of an illness lie in the past, the distant past of another life. Sometimes an illness can be more of a gift than a curse. As near as I can tell, the truth of this can be found in our attitudes and in our willingness to acknowledge that any problem can be used as an opportunity for growth and learning. Stories like this, incredible stories of the power of love, have taught me to reserve judgment. We cannot know the real why of things, but we can strive for the healing balm forgiveness and understanding offer. The illustration here of one soul sacrificing for another happens more often than you might think.

Sample F

I will wrap up this chapter with a series of two questions asked by a Canadian woman in her late thirties. "Was there a significant past-life connection between me and Jon-Jacques?"

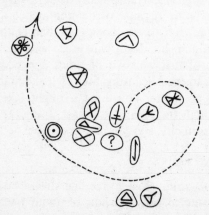

THE CAST

My eyes spiraled around the female question stone in a clockwise fashion. Impressions from within me placed this woman's life in France during the middle 1800s, a female life. Observe how Negativity points directly at Fire, indicating a rigid and confining childhood spent in a religious family unit. Change signifies that she left as soon as possible and was befriended by a man she fell in love with (Man, Love). Woman and Home I felt covered her involvement in her new environment and the status she achieved as a strong, confident woman. The more successful she became (Money, and as related to Gifts, Comfort, Beneficial Gain), the more at risk she was (Confusion), until people finally turned against her (Marriage, Conflict).

INTERPRETATION

My answer was yes. What I described was a French life, quite provincial, in which her duties included both a house and a yard to tend. Intuitively, I felt her parents were strict Catholics: no nonsense, no fantasies, no time for imagination. She had an unusually bright, quick mind and an excellent memory. She was given an offer to move to a larger city and work as an apprentice to a shopkeeper. Once she left home, she never returned (notice how Change divides her youth from her adulthood). There was a small room on the premises where she stayed, with a straw mattress for a bed. The arrangement was perfect for her, and she thrived in the city. She loved all the people, fashions, animals, fancy carts, carriages, and activities. She attended various classes when possible, became literate, and excelled in math. She had so many ideas on how to improve the shop's business that she became an "assistant manager," urging the owner to open up similar shops in other towns. Business flourished, along with her worth. The two fell in love, even though the owner was married and had numerous grown children. They did share in sexual relations on occasion, but she refused to become a mistress. The unique arrangement she and the owner enjoyed confused his wife and family. They assumed the worst and filed serious charges against her, demanding a hearing before a tribunal. Everything she had accomplished was used against her, even her ability at mathematical calculations. ("Decent women don't do this, you know.") The trial was a sham, the lies vicious. The owner (Jon-Jacques in this life) retired to the background and, like a wimp, said nothing in her defense. She was imprisoned during the trial, but banished shortly thereafter. I sensed she fled to Spain. With no money and no friends, she became a barmaid and drifted into prostitution, choking to death in an alcoholic fit on a dusty floor.

"What is our relationship to be like in this life?" my questioner asked, noting that she and this man were just friends for now.

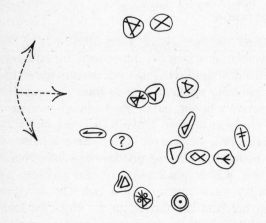

THE CAST

Change, decidedly alone yet next to the female question stone, tells me the theme of this cast is transformation. Follow the course of my eye movements as they radiated to the right (Fire, Comfort nearby, Beneficial Gain, Man, Negativity pointed near the man's head as if a sign of shame, a guilty conscience), to the top (Love, Woman, Conflict, Gifts, Confusion, looking like a recent affair gone sour), and to the bottom (Home, Marriage, Money, like a repeat of their previous-life involvement).

INTERPRETATION

I had no doubt that the two of them could be friends. It seemed to me that he was just coming out of a love relationship with another woman, or was still somewhat involved, but the chemistry wasn't right and the affair was going nowhere. Thus, his emotional nature would be unreliable. The two of them could become more than friends someday, but I doubted it. The better choice, as I saw it, would be to ask his advice about her business (she is a business consultant/trainer). His ideas would be good ones (Fire, Beneficial Gain), and she could use the assistance. Plus, she could help him as well. It was obvious to me that a great deal of subconscious interplay would tend to undergird anything they did—on her part, feelings of betrayal and abandonment (you owe me); and with him, a sense of shame and guilt (I need to pay you back). Since the purpose of their relationship was one of transformation, I suggested that she facilitate the forgiveness that was needed here by engaging in what they both knew best—helping each other make money and expand markets—so their past could be healed and their present made whole.

RESPONSE AND RESULTS

The woman simply smiled and said, "I thought so." She walked away displaying a sense of relief, almost as if a burden had been lifted and she could believe in herself again.

Herman Melville, author of the classic *Moby Dick,* once said: "We cannot live for ourselves alone. Our lives are connected by a thousand invisible threads, and along these sympathetic fibers, our actions run as causes and return to us as results."

Reincarnational story lines illuminate Melville's statement, giving perspective to puzzles, offering reason to what seems ridiculous. Whether they are true in the strictest sense or not, people are healed and helped by them—and that's what counts.

CHAPTER SIX

Goddess Wisdoms

Since 1978, I have been privileged to teach thousands of people The Way of A Cast using Goddess Runes. During this time I have discovered people who, in not understanding mind and spirit, turned divinatory art forms into circus sideshows. All manner of issues surfaced for these people, from the ethics of fortune-telling to the problem of possible possession by disincarnates (bodiless beings). I have also found that a few simple concerns about rune casting consistently confuse people and often require further elaboration.

Because of these discoveries, I would like to share some suggestions and advice—goddess wisdoms—that may help you to establish and maintain perspective. The willingness to seek a grander vision of the larger whole can lead to *either* self-deception or discernment. Thus, double-checking what you think you know, insisting on clarity, will guide you more truly than the so-called "enlightened" (i.e., those people who appear to be further advanced in their spiritual development than they really are).

Here are some goddess wisdoms I would offer, arranged by category:

1. Secrets of Interpreting a Cast
Three keys will unlock the secrets of interpreting any rune

cast: eyesight discipline, pattern recognition, and receptivity to intuitive promptings.

A) I cannot emphasize enough that interpretation begins with the question stone. Train yourself to see it first. The scattering of runic glyphs in a cast has no value if the questioner's energy is not central to the cast. The question stone represents the questioner's energy; it honors that individual and whatever is the *real* question at hand, be it spoken or not. The question stone is your link to the inner depths of the energy that is reflected before you (the individual and his or her issues). From the central focus it affords, allow your eyes to radiate out or spiral around, catching in your sight the locations of the various glyphs. Be aware of any runic glyph that skips away or refuses to cooperate, for it is asking to be excused from the cast.

B) Teach yourself to look for an overall pattern to the cast. A pattern may not always be present, but the majority of casts will have one. This overall pattern is quite literally the theme of the cast, influencing the direction and import of any message the runes might convey.

Go back through Chapter Four (present-life samples) and see if you can find any casts that have overall, central patterns. Actually, they all do, but some are more pronounced than others. Take, for instance, Sample B. In this cast, the chalice shape is plainly visible. It is the wedding chalice that the questioner wishes to drink from. Notice, though, that Man is suspended midway over the open cup of the chalice, directly in line with Conflict, Negativity, Change, and Money. Comfort and the question stone to the right side reveal the only "right" solution to the question. This is certainly an example of a very powerful overall pattern with an equally powerful theme. Another example of such a striking design is Sample E. Yet overall patterns can sometimes be elusive and difficult to recognize, as Sample H proved to me until I finally saw the "square" that revealed the cast's true meaning. Yet in this sample I could have ascertained that the "H" within the square stood for "hard" or "Honda" or "hindrance," equally valid clues that would have led to the same conclusion.

In most of the sample casts illustrated in this book, I have left it up to you to decide whether or not there is an overall pattern to the cast, and whether smaller patterns exist within it. If I explained every little detail of each cast and what I think it means, you would be denied the opportunity to recognize what is there yourself. Ample hints are given. The rest is for you to decide.

In The Way of A Cast, meaning emerges from patterns, not necessarily from individual glyphs. A pattern, remember, is a symbol or design that blends together many parts to form a whole. So always be sure to look for patterns—including any overall design as well as major and/or minor groupings. Train yourself to widen your view. Discipline your eyes to connect or link together the glyphs you see.

C) The success of any form of divination depends on one's receptivity to the process of intuitive guidance. Intuition is that subtle wee voice at the inner core of our being. It is our conscience, the part of us "that knows that it knows"—perhaps the very voice of our own soul, and of every other soul. Sometimes intuition speaks, for we seem to hear an actual "voice"; sometimes it nudges, like a gentle "push" from behind; and sometimes it expresses itself through the gut or the feeling structure of our emotions and senses. Science tells us that intuition is a product of the right hemisphere of our brain. Psychics say that it is the initial entry point to psychism itself and the development of psychic abilities. Whatever it is called or thought to be, intuition is an invaluable skill that is necessary, I believe, for a healthy, well-rounded life. We are not balanced or whole without it.

Men, by the way, are just as intuitive as women. The only difference is that women more readily accept their intuitive abilities, while men usually do everything they can to deny them. This has more to do with cultural stigmas than with natural receptivity.

The Way of A Cast nurtures and develops intuition and promotes synergy (whole-brain functioning). It teaches you how to use both brain hemispheres more effectively and efficiently as you learn to trust the abilities you develop. This type of free-form casting depends on the intuitive process to work. No opportunity exists in this system for a person to lean on the security of rules, regulations, layouts, or formats.

Through pure spontaneity and the immediacy of the moment, one is obliged to surrender to the power of love and truth, the wisdom of the inner self, the Greater Self, The God Within. Because surrender of the ego (releasing the outer self or personality facade) is so necessary, protection of the inner self is paramount. That's why the ancients held rituals of cleansing and attunement before practicing divinatory arts. To ensure proper reception, they practiced proper preparation. Shortcuts were not allowed.

2. Historical Context

Rune use re-creates a sense of innocence and brings to mind a time in history when the human race was young. Some people, though, especially those who use the more "modern" Futhark, often try to reestablish cultural mannerisms and rituals long since discarded, i.e. that of Celts and Vikings. This can be fun, and it can be tremendously rewarding. But what is known about this epoch in runic history can be tricky, tricky in the sense that overreliance on such information can result in a mind-set so dogmatic that spontaneity is lost. Spontaneity is what makes rune casting unique and gives divination its mystery. You cannot limit the limitless and still have ready access to the creative spirit you are trying to reach.

For this reason, I pass along the following advice about trying too hard to mimic historical facts and fantasies:

> We don't go back to the past—we reach back to the past and bring what is helpful and useful into our modern society and into our modern lives. We have to live now; we can't live then. If we try to live then, we are in trouble.[22]

These words of counsel were spoken by E. Otha Wingo, Ph.D., during a 1984 interview conducted by Peter Young on radio station KKON, Kealakekua, Hawaii. Wingo is director of Huna Research, Inc., headquartered in Missouri, and a college professor of ancient languages. His caution related to ancient philosophical and divinatory systems is worth heeding. (Huna, by the way, is a practical system of spirituality developed centuries ago in the Hawaiian islands. Although the word *Huna* means "secret," the system it espouses is applicable to modern lifestyles.)

No matter how hard a person strives for historical authenticity and no matter how thorough his or her research, any runes used today will still be viewed through modern eyes and tossed with muscles powered by the present moment.

Wise is the person who learns from the past, but foolish is the one who clings to it.

3. Overuse and Misuse

You can use runes too often. Any divinatory skill can become a crutch leading to dependence, false illusions, and addiction. When you ask the same question over and over again, you chain yourself to the "merry-go-round" of indecision. Even masking your concerns by rewording your requests for the same guidance will, if done repeatedly, net you no more than distortion or confusion.

We can sabotage ourselves by our own impatience. Our egos can take over and overwhelm the divinatory process from sheer force of will, thus ensuring that our own self-centered prophecies will be the outcome. It is amazing to me how often people receive in "guidance" only what they want to receive. This is self-deception—the biggest entrapment of all!

You cannot hurry divinatory processes, for they are based on feeling and sensing, not on conscious thinking or the passion of desire. The purpose of their use is guidance, not ego strokes. The true power of divination comes from communion with the Greater Self. Complexities of ritual and perceptions of urgency can detract from this goal.

One woman I met had reworded her same question over and over again, casting up to three times per day, day after day, for more than a week, and then wondered why she felt so irritable and frustrated. Of course she felt that way. How many times must a person be given the same information before overload occurs and the nervous system rebels?

Runes cannot make decisions. They cannot decide the future. They and any other divinatory tool can only impart information. The rest is up to you. Make your choices, act on them, and then face the consequences responsibly.

4. Question Stones and Sexual Energy

Question stones represent more than just gender; they relate to the physical makeup of sexual energy. Archaeologists have conjectured that the sex acts practiced as part of ancient rituals probably had more to do with symbolism than eroticism, or even a belief in the afterlife. That symbolism seemed to portray male energy as the positive pole of vibrational attraction; female, the negative. The two in union, as signified by sexual intercourse and orgasm, were indicative of an energy charge.

Keeping this in mind, one can reexamine stories told by the lore masters of old and recognize in those stories thinly veiled treatises on a "science of sex." Anthropologists have noticed the same thing; so have other professionals. It's as if our ancestors understood that sexual energy could be used as a model to help them harness and direct opposing poles of energy attraction. Knowledge of such a model may have enabled them to accomplish the great feats they did, feats that we in the age of jet planes and moon rockets still puzzle about. There exists today a whole body of research that delves into this ancient "science of sex," for some suspect that it holds the secret as to why megalithic monuments were built and how healing and fertility rites were performed.

This understanding of sexual energy as opposing poles of attraction is central to The Way of A Cast, and important to other forms of divination as well. Because of this, I want to clarify what is traditionally meant by sexual energy in terms of "male" and "female" expressions of that energy.

Based on the Taoist principle of yin for female energy and the principle of yang for male energy, here is an exercise for you to do:

** Stand straight, with your feet flat on the floor and your arms held skyward. Clasp your hands together as far over your head as possible. Then, keeping your hands clasped, try to pull your hands apart. Strain to pull them apart while keeping them firmly clasped together. This steady holding together is what yang energy feels like.

** Again, stand straight with your feet flat on the floor, your arms held skyward, and your hands clasped together as far over your head as possible. This time, however, when you try to separate your clasped hands, allow them to slip apart. This is yin energy. It is that which was once together but is now pulled apart; it yields.

In the classic sense, sexual energies are defined according to principle and polarity:

Yang Energy

The undivided ego—which seeks ever to divide. Objective, mental, self-confident, firm, analytical, assertive. Characterized by a positive energy charge and a descending current (from outside in). Carries within it the potential for yin. Symbolically considered masculine. Represented by a straight (usually vertical) vision line within the inner eye.

Yin Energy

The divided ego—which seeks ever to unite. Subjective, emotional, compassionate, yielding, intuitive, passive. Characterized by a negative energy charge and an ascending current (from inside out). Carries within it the potential for yang. Symbolically considered feminine. Represented by a curved (usually horizontal) vision line within the inner eye.

Also in the classic sense, orgasms and enlightenment (lesser and greater ecstasy) demonstrate how polarities of energy combine:

Orgasm

The ego merges with self—union, the pleasure of released energies, access to undifferentiated power. Characterized by scattered charges from either or both energy currents. Temporary satisfaction. Symbolically considered a physical bonding. Represented by a multidirectional (often spiraling) vision line within the inner eye.

Enlightenment

The ego-self reunifies with the Greater Self—convergence, reunion, pure ecstasy. Transcends the realms of energy; access to the omnipotent power of God (deity). Characterized by ascending and descending energy currents meeting with equal force and creating a light flash. Lasting satisfaction. Symbolically considered a spiritual transformation. Represented by an all-encompassing vision line, transcending the inner eye.

It is reasonable to assume that the reality of sexual energies and the experience of orgasm helped ancient peoples to define and understand life processes, even creation itself. Enlightenment has been known across the ages as the ultimate orgasm, whereby an individual surrendered to and was overwhelmed by a power greater than anything from the sensory world. And this power has always been known to free individuals from earthly attachments and introduce them to the truth of real knowledge and real power—an experience of Oneness. Since enlightenment transfigures and transforms so visibly, people who experienced it were often revered as wise ones and chosen for leadership, guidance, or counseling roles.

5. Mind Development

The Way of A Cast reflects whatever level of mind development and maturity you have attained. This is also true of other forms of divination. Here are some examples of the ways divination can be viewed by those of various mind-sets:

- If you are selfish or vengeful, the guidance you seek can be manipulative or controlling, and trick you into thinking you are more powerful than you really are.

- If you are still childish in your reasoning, your interpretations can tend to be overly literal and rigid.

- Should play be your only interest in divination—the fun of a unique hobby—the guidance received is often unreliable or nonsensical.

- If you are excessively mechanistic or analytical, divinatory tools will have little value to you, and will seem to be a confusing array of practices designed to cheat and enslave the unsuspecting.

- Should religious fundamentalism be your passion, divination will appear to be "the devil's work" and a sure-fire path to damnation—until you reread the Christian Bible and discover that, besides warnings against the misuse of such skills, this sacred text also contains a veritable digest of divination at its best.

- To the psychic, one divination skill can appear the same as another, valuable only as "proof" of psychic competence.

- For the openly curious yet more mature, divination often becomes a way of reflecting back to the inner self whatever is being projected—of creating a psychological portrait helpful for inner growth.

- With those who have developed an understanding of spirituality, divination will indeed signal "divinity" in the way it accesses more expansive realms of mind and spirit, and in the way it fosters respect for the sacredness of all life-forms.

- But for the mystic, ceremonies, rituals, objects, and tools cease to have much, if any, value. Gnosis (knowing) surfaces for these people, enabling them to have more direct contact with whatever guidance or information might be helpful. Divinatory methods may seem unnecessary to them, or perhaps like an old "toy" long since forgotten.

Divination can and will be whatever you make of it. In truth, divination is but a simple skill that has only one function—to access other realms of knowledge for the purpose of gaining information. Any tool (object) that might be used as part of the divining process makes no difference in and of itself, for it is the attitude and personal preference of *the one who uses the tool* that determines the validity *of* the tool.

6. Psychic Possession

It is possible for a disembodied being or an energy mass to gain entry to and/or control of your body sometimes, seemingly without your permission. This is called "psychic possession." Don't tolerate this invasion. No ghostly being, thoughtform, or any other "thing" has the right to invade your privacy and your life without permission. Just because a disincarnate or disembodied being might claim to be your guide or friend or an emissary from "higher" spiritual realms does not mean it's the truth. A disincarnate—someone who is dead (without a body)—or a spirit form can claim anything. These disincarnates, and lower astral beings (negative thoughtforms or spirits still attached to the earthplane), are quite real, but more of a nuisance than a threat. They can tempt you, proposition you, seem friendly enough, provide accurate guidance for a while, make you feel important or needed—all for the purpose of cajoling you into letting them stick around. If you are lonely, feeling impotent or guilty, lost or unloved, needful of more attention and personal power, or perhaps on drugs or alcohol, the "deal" they offer may seem too good to refuse. *Just say no!*

Possession by another entity or energy form denies you your own free will. It is not worth the price of any promise.

Possession eventually drains vital energy from the host body and destroys both health and safety.

Negative energy feeds lower astral forms, allowing them to grow more powerful. Positive energy either dissolves these astral forms into nothingness or renders them powerless. You are not at their mercy, nor are you their victim. You have the power to take charge. It is your life and you are in control. Not everyone who alters his or her consciousness faces the prospect of possession, but if you do, here are a few steps you can take:

** Do not allow yourself to feel or express any negative emotions when the "being" is present, for negativity can betray you or weaken your strength. Remember, you are in charge. Think positively. You have nothing to fear.

** Assert yourself and state your right to exist free of interference from anyone, or from anything from other levels of existence, at any time.

** Affirm your identity as a child of God. You are protected by God. You are divine and whole and filled with God's Holy Light. Positively know this! See Light filling your entire being and surrounding you in a bubble of protective love.

** Command the spirit being, disincarnate, thoughtform, or whatever to be gone at once—totally gone, permanently and forever gone, now!

** See the "being" disappear into the radiance of God's Holy Light. Know that this is true. Feel it. Affirm it.

** State that you are free, and that the air is clear and cleansed. Know that there is only life and love and joy because there is only God. Nothing and no one can violate this truth. Affirm divine order.

Sometimes problems with psychic possession are more the result of poor diet or lack of self-esteem than of any invasion by disincarnates or energy forms. It may not be the dead who should concern you, but rather the way you live your life. Have a good health checkup. Pay special attention to your vitamin/mineral intake, your hormone balance, regular exercise, and the consumption of complete proteins. Make certain you are assimilating what you ingest, and take steps to strengthen your immune system. Healthy, happy people with positive self-images virtually never have problems with possession.

7. Channeling

The type of channeling that is popular today was once referred to as "trance mediumship." Trance mediumship involves an individual inviting, then allowing, a disembodied spirit being or spirit entity to use his or her vocal chords and body energy for the purpose of speaking and/or moving around in the physical world. This arrangement is based on temporary or occasional usage, and is agreed upon by all parties concerned. You can employ various levels of the trance state to reach numerous dimensions or realms of involvement. As is always true of any endeavor, mediumship—whether in trance or not—can be positive, negative, or a little of both. More often than not, it is the result of either the ego-self or the Greater Self overshadowing the individual's personality. Even if a disincarnate, spirit guide, or transcendent entity should make contact, what then flows forth from the medium or channeler is seldom anything other than what could have been gained through the time-honored practices of meditation and prayer.

What we now call channeling was originally used as a means to contact the dead and prove there is life after death. Such channeled contacts did indeed produce provocative information, some of which was later verified. For example, the entire Xerox photocopy technique was credited by its inventor, Chester F. Carlson, as having come from spirit beings channeled through a trance medium.

Real channeling, however, covers far more than an emergence or manifestation of disincarnates. Channeling ability can signal: mind-to-mind telepathy, including telepathy with animals; contact with other forms of intelligence such as elements, minerals, and plants; a visit from the proverbial Greek muses who, as legend tells us, inspire, motivate, and tease us into peaks of creativity and flashes of insight; and the influence of thoughtforms, your own or from others, as we digest and process various types of input.

If voices or thoughts other than your own seek your attention or try to express themselves through you, use the following chart comparing energies from different levels as a guide before you decide to accept or reject what is happening.

LESSER MIND *The Voice of Ego Personality Level*	GREATER MIND *The Voice of Spirit Soul Level*
flatters	informs
commands	suggests
demands	guides
tests	nudges
chooses for you	leaves choice to you
imprisons	empowers
promotes dependency	promotes independence
intrudes	respects
pushes	supports
excludes	includes

LESSER MIND *The Voice of Ego* *Personality Level*	GREATER MIND *The Voice of Spirit* *Soul Level*
is status-oriented	is free and open
insists on obedience	encourages growth and development
often claims ultimate authority	recognizes a greater power, or God
offers shortcuts	offers integration
seeks personal gratification	affirms divine order along with the good of the whole

Remember, whatever you project returns to you. Channeling information from another source does *not* exempt you from taking responsibility for the information that is delivered. It is up to *you* to double-check, or somehow verify or affirm the validity and value of what is channeled through you. Our rational skills are just as important as our intuitive skills. Seldom will wisdom emerge until both are used in concert with each other.

And especially remember: anyone who claims to be the only source of a spiritual revelation is either a fool or a fake. Channeling is a route through which anything can pass, and that's all it is. There are no guarantees in its use.

I believe the reason that channeling is so popular today is the gentleness it offers, enabling one to touch the holiness of being. Problems arise when the contacted source is automatically claimed to be some "limitless font of truth," when in fact *the response* elicited in the channeler and in those affected by what's channeled is more important than what is said. People want to feel important and humble at the same time. Channeling is one way to address that need.

8. Fortune-telling and the Issue of Power

Fortune-telling—predicting what will definitely happen in the future—is impossible if divinatory tools are used properly.

Probabilities can be surmised, but little else. The true purpose of divination is to seek and gain information from a broader perspective, which involves detaching oneself from the given situation and any emotional investment in its outcome. Divination involves relaxing, releasing ego needs, and surrendering to a higher or more expansive state of consciousness. These steps are necessary because the answer to any question always resides within the question itself, yet at the next level up in vibration.

Information gained through divination offers objective viewpoints, not absolutes. Every time a new choice is made, the future changes and all the players on the stage of life shift positions.

However, *the goal* of our particular life, our purpose for being here, does seem to be unchangeable. It is how we achieve our goal or fail in our effort that is entirely flexible.

Free will, then, is the guarantee and the birthright of every soul to express. Even if we seem unable to change life's circumstances, we can always change our response to those circumstances. Changing our response has a way of eventually changing what happens to us. Caution: telling someone that a specific event will definitely occur often programs that individual to expect it. (Expectation is the forerunner of action, setting in motion the forces of attraction that draw to us what we expect.)

No one has the right to try and program another person. We can attempt to influence each other. We can teach, lead, guide, inspire, and motivate; but we cannot rob others of their power, their power of free will. Since what is given out returns, to enslave another is to enslave ourself; to manipulate or try to control another is to weaken our own power base.

Accurate predictions are often more indicative of how easy it is to program people than they are as proof of any fortune-teller's skill.

Fortune-telling is wrapped up in the issue of power—what it is and how it is handled. The word "power" is derived from the Latin word for "to be able" and refers to every person's right to claim identity, recognition, and worthiness. True power inspires rather than forces; gives examples, not orders; guides, not directs; motivates, not limits; empowers, not imprisons. True power is a gentle radiance ... ever expanding, ever including, ever uplifting ... the harmonic balance between our inner and outer worlds, the activity of love.

9. Magic

The general public still equates fortune-telling with magic. But what do we mean by "magic"?

There are three basic types. In modern parlance, the word "magic" supposedly refers to "the power of influence," and is recognizable by the "color" of its purpose and usage:

White Magic—spirit-based, for the purpose of healing one's self and others; emphasizes growth and guardianship; enhances, charms, protects.

> USAGES—lighting candles, burning incense, setting out flower-petal potpourri, hanging wind chimes or crystals for the purpose of creating a certain mood or outcome; using herbs for healing or for cooking; protecting natural environments and legacies; working for the good fortune and success of the deserving; creating feasts and fairs for public enjoyment and edification.

Black Magic—ego-based, for the purpose of adding to one's self-importance; emphasizes possessions and status; indulges, exploits, enslaves.

> USAGES—employing trickery or deceit to make oneself look better, fool someone, or cause something to happen; seeking to control others through willpower; "arranging" recognition and advancement instead of earning it; threatening anyone not liked or wishing another harm; taking over without permission, buying loy-

alty, demanding one's own way; lusting for more, insatiable appetites.

Gray Magic—belief-based, for the purpose of acquiring attention or imposing a point of view; emphasizes wishful thinking and cultural fixations; entices, coerces, programs.

> USAGES—telling "white" lies to avoid facing the truth; engaging in "quick fixes" that compromise integrity and in spiritual "shortcuts" that bypass integration; assuming what someone wants without asking; helping people who do not want or need help; justifying hostile actions by claiming "righteous indignation"; maneuvering events and outcomes to fit personal agendas; false advertising, half-truths, programming.

As there are different types of magic, there are also various ways to regard the term. For instance, "magic" can refer to attraction, mystery, charisma, awe, wonder, seduction, hocus-pocus, trickery, evil, enslavement. In the strictest sense, however, none of the depictions I have shared with you so far are true. "Magic" actually traces back to the traditions of ancient Babylonia and Persia and the concept of "receptivity," originally written as "magno." "Magnet" and "magnetic" are derived from the term magno, as are "magi" and "magic." Thus we have:

Real Magic—feeling-based, for the purpose of establishing an open and accepting mood; emphasizes receptivity and sensitivity; enables, readies, resonates.

Our forebears understood that when someone was receptive and sensitive enough, that person could then draw to him or her all manner of unique or desirable happenings with little or no effort, almost as if "charmed" (possessed of magic). Today, receptivity is regarded as a willingness to receive and an openness that is both responsive and nonjudgmental. These qualities are a must if one is to explore, invent, create, or exhibit the sureness of faith that trust and joy foster. Developing receptivity (real magic) is the purpose behind all ritual.

And there's one more:

Soul Magic—source-based, for the purpose of learning through experience so the soul can evolve; emphasizes self-empowerment and personal responsibility; uplifts, frees, brings together in wholeness.

As you can well suppose, we are all practitioners of some type of magic. We could not progress through life if this were not so.

10. Sensitivity and Balance

The Way of A Cast is one of the most delightful methods I know for developing and learning to trust your own intuitive and psychic ability. It is immediate, demonstrative, and open-ended, thus providing an easy way to gauge progress and improvement. The subconscious mind, and perhaps even the superconscious mind, is readily accessed by practicing the skill. Traditionally, it is said that the mind consists of conscious, subconscious, and superconscious levels. Here is how I define these levels:

The Conscious Level feels wide awake and alert. It collects and interprets facts and details from objective reality. It is associated with the left hemisphere of the brain.
The Subconscious Level feels dreamy and detached. It sifts and intuits creative possibilities from subjective reality. It is associated with the right hemisphere of the brain.
The Superconscious Level feels wise and knowing, as if it is connected to larger expanses of mind such as group, race, or universal mind. It infuses guidance from collective reality. It is associated with the limbic system of the brain as relates to higher brain functioning.

There is nothing mystical, religious, or even fearsome about altering one's state of consicousness. We do it all the time whether we realize it or not. Altering consciousess is a natural process; divination as a way to tune in to things psychic is based on this fact. Psychism represents a vast world of mystery for most people, as it envelops the subtle realms of subjective reality. Psychic abilities enable us to enter this "other" world and look around. Skills of the psychic operate like antennae, extending the natural reach of faculties that are normal to us.

It has been my experience that although psychism appears as different abilities and manifestations, it is really various expressions of the same mechanism, which can be controlled and trained. It is like a basic talent that can be directed into numerous channels. Call it a skill, if you will. Just as with any other skill, it can be ignored, used as it is, or developed and improved with practice. It can also emerge seemingly full-blown at birth. Quite simply put, to be alive is to be psychic. Psychic ability is more akin to breathing than it is to riding a broomstick, despite some popular attitudes to the contrary. But as with anything else in life, *use determines value*. Self-discipline makes a difference, and so does focus—because wherever you put your attention is where you put your power. By focusing on such attributes as the greater good, divine order, and wholeness, you can ensure the healthy unfolding of psychism. By focusing on God, all levels of life automatically begin to balance in ways that lead to the highest good of all concerned.

Native Americans say, "Walk in balance," because they know that balance (the integration of our physical, mental, emotional, and spiritual selves) is the secret of a life well lived. It is not who we are that matters, but what we have become; not what we possess, but what we have shared or given away. The bottom line is not profit; it is service *plus* long-term investment in the education and upliftment of others.

It is my hope that these goddess wisdoms prove helpful to you, and provide a sound base from which you can determine for yourself what has value and what doesn't. The realms of spirit are not frightful, and the depths of divination need not be mysterious. When we practice divinatory skills, we are really exploring our own capacities and potentials to stretch beyond our apparent limitations. It is a way to reconnect with joy.

CHAPTER SEVEN

Memories and Mind

While I was researching the origin of runes, I uncovered more than I had bargained for. Modern technology and a new breed of highly skilled professionals have turned our purported knowledge of ancient times upside down, and have revealed as fiction some of what was once thought to be fact. As we access more artifacts and reinvestigate former findings, the puzzle pieces of the past have begun to fit a different mold—one that is far more fascinating and thought-provoking than previously believed.

While this is not a book of history per se, if you will bear with me, I think you will find taking yet another excursion into times past will be worth doing. It may help clarify why so many people recognize runic glyphs as if they were part of their own personal memories. By looking backward, we can better understand the present, and maybe even how life itself evolves.

Consider that geoscientists measuring acoustic waves generated by earthquakes have produced scans that show remnants of continents and other structures in and near the earth's core. Also consider that recent satellite photographs reveal surface features on earth indicative of advanced civilizations so old that no records exist to identify them; that in all probability South America, Africa, India, Australia, and Antarctica were once part of the same great land mass.

New dating techniques have created an embarrassing abundance of artifacts that defy previous scholarship. For example, there are acid batteries that are over two thousand years old; evidence of the use of electricity was found as early as the Sumerian culture; the alloy aluminum was commonly used in fourth-century Chinese art; the process of iron milling (covering iron with silicon) has turned out to be thousands of years old; modern-looking human skulls are at least one-hundred thousand years old; a spark plug encased in rock dates back five-hundred thousand years; a sandal print of a right foot stepping on trilo-bites dates from six million years ago (humans weren't supposed to be around then); and a human-made metal cube has been found embedded in a block of coal over twelve million years old. (Artifacts, that do not fit "acceptable" science are called "anomalies." Refer to Footnote 23 for more information.)

Such anomalies nullify the idea of a progressive linear his-tory, evidencing instead sweeping cycles of brilliant ascension followed by catastrophic decline. As one anonymous archaeolo-gist noted, "Always there are Noahs, survivors to seed the next cycle."

Among the "primitive" remnants still existing, we have the Great Pyramid at Giza, from which the earth's size and shape can be calculated, including the degree of equatorial bulge and polar flatness, to a precision matched only by today's satellite measurements. Popular opinion dates the Pyramid at about 3000 B.C., but most professionals feel that this date is still imprecise. So how old is it? Who built it, and why? Even today, we could not duplicate this architectural feat.

Then we have a most unusual poem, an epic of ancient India called the *Mahabharata*. The world's longest poetic master-piece, it consists of one-hundred thousand stanzas. Although parts of the poem can be traced to 3102 B.C., its oral traditions are claimed to stem from ten thousand years ago. In the last of its three major sections, it describes what was probably a nu-clear holocaust, complete with the dropping of bombs from airborne craft, mushroom clouds, scorched earth, and vaporized people and animals. Of two sites bombed by the "Rods of Brahmin" in this poem, one of them, the south-central Deccan

Valley, still exhibits evidence today of vitrification (surface melt
from sudden extreme heat) and harbors bones that have been
found to register radiation fifty times above normal levels for
that area. A huge mountain of glass in the Brazilian jungle is
said to have resulted from that same holocaust, which supposedly wiped out many ancient cities and the lost continent of
Atlantis as well.

Could Nagasaki and Hiroshima be repeats of a far more ancient folly? Recorded in what we know of history are endless
examples of such catastrophic destruction. Legends and myths
from every culture on earth describe the rise of advanced societies and their devastating declines that swept away all traces of
their existence save for a few struggling survivors. Nothing
remains but memories and the telling of tales.

It has been my experience that history repeats itself only
when people fail to learn from it, yet the cycles referred to here
cover time frames so vast that one wonders how learning can
occur when the knowledge to support that learning seems to be
nonexistent. Is there anything that explains this? Could we as
intelligent beings have forgotten or refused to honor other facets
of our intelligence?

The answer is yes, *our memories*!

Dreams and visions of other lives, other worlds, other civilizations, other times—persisting in the modern psyche of humankind—are all so strikingly similar that childhood fantasies,
cultural traditions, and even reincarnational memories do not
fully explain them away.

In *The Letters of J.R.R. Tolkien,* edited by Humphrey Carpenter with the assistance of Christopher Tolkien, various passages
reveal some surprising things about J.R.R. Tolkien and what
propelled him to produce his many books on Middle Earth,
which are one of the greatest treasures of fantasy/myth ever
written. Tolkien said:

Yet always I had the sense of recording what was already
"there" . . . that I was not inventing but reporting . . . For
when Faramir speaks of his private vision of the Great

Wave, he speaks for me. That vision and dream has been
ever with me ... What I might call my Atlantis-haunting.
This legend or myth or dim memory of some ancient history has always troubled me. In sleep I had the dreadful
dream of the ineluctable Wave, either coming out of the
quiet sea, or coming in towering over the green inlands.
It still occurs occasionally, though now exorcized by writing about it. It always ends by surrender, and I awake
gasping out of deep water ... I began an abortive book
of time-travel of which the end was to be the presence of
my hero in the drowning of Atlantis. This was to be called
NÚMENOR, Land in the West ... Though it is only in
reading the work myself (with criticisms in mind) that I
become aware of the dominance of the theme of Death
... that the "message" was the hideous peril of confusing
true "immortality" with limitless serial longevity. Freedom from Time, and clinging to Time.[24]

Surely there must exist somewhere, somehow, a kind of
"central storage bank" of collective memory—invisible, ethe-
ric, and accessible subconsciously or consciously—which contains imprints and impressions from all that was, all that is,
and, perhaps, all that might ever be. Freud labeled this possible
storage bank "racial memory" and Jung called it "the collective unconscious." Metaphysically, it is often referred to as
"universal mind," or "mass mind," or the "Akashic Records." However labeled, it seems to be a "place" or perhaps
a "field" where group memories and various types of accumulated data are stored.

Recognizing and investigating the validity of information
from this memory source is as important to the understanding
of history and human development as the procurement and
study of physical evidence. *Neither source of information is
complete without the other.*

Other archetypal reservoirs of memory may also exist, layers
of them, each for different reasons and different purposes. We
know, for instance, that molecular DNA ribbons direct the me-

chanics of physical reproduction, but what directs the DNA? Chemical interactions within DNA do not dictate evolution. So what does?

Rupert Sheldrake, an English plant biologist, has come up with an answer he describes in his book, *A New Science of Life.*[25] It is well worth taking time to consider. Sheldrake theorizes that primary sources of mass memory do indeed exist, residing in nonenergetic field currents that permeate all levels of existence. He names these "morphogenetic" (Greek for "form beginning") fields, or "M-fields." According to Sheldrake, these M-fields direct the shape, development, and basic behavior of all living species and systems, functioning as invisible blueprints or connecting memories, if you will, linking any member of a given species or system with its fellows while supplying a ready bank of accumulated information that members can instinctively and automatically draw from or contribute to. M-fields, then, constantly change and evolve as individual members learn and grow. Changes in the field, however, are not always instantaneous. It seems a certain threshold must first be reached before the entire field is affected. (Although the threshold figure is unknown, some estimate that it is around ten percent.) Once the number of changed individual members reaches that threshold, field activation occurs and all members, no matter where they are located or how much time has lapsed, are then stimulated to copy or express the change. Incredible as this sounds, all attempts to disprove Sheldrake's bizarre theory have only added to the mountains of evidence supporting it.

The small European bird called the blue tit illustrates how Sheldrake believes M-fields work. This little warbler discovered how to open foil caps from milk bottles left on doorsteps and drink off the top cream. Once the blue tits within a small area had taught one another the trick and then mastered it, suddenly all the other blue tits across the entire European continent were doing the same thing, without benefit of either direct exposure or teaching. The same thing happened with Macaca Fuscata monkeys on an island off the northern coast of Japan. One monkey discovered how to wash freshly dug sweet potatoes before eating them and then taught this to some other monkeys. Soon, after most of the island monkeys had learned and mastered the new trick, all the other monkeys of that species on the other islands and even on the mainland were doing it, too. In both these cases, physical contact between the various species members was not possible, yet the new skills were transmitted to every member as if by "magic."

It is important to note here that human history is crammed with examples duplicating those found among animals—cases where ideas and skills have spread to far-flung corners of the globe without physical evidence to support how such information was communicated. Because of new dating procedures, we now know that the possibility of one human culture physically influencing another is different from what was previously believed.

Consider these puzzles. Sumerians and Babylonians "suddenly" started practicing advanced astronomy and geometry *after* mysterious builders of northern European passage graves *had already* developed and perfected both sciences in mound construction. Romans erected aqueducts and complex irrigation and plumbing systems *after* these were in wide use by Olmecs and Mayans on the opposite side of the globe. Yoga postures were *routinely* practiced in the Crimea and across Old Europe *before* being "invented" in India. Trial by jury and democratic codes of law were *common* in many areas of deepest Africa *before* "civilized" empires in Asia and Europe "originated" such ideas. Rituals and priesthood practices of Celtic Druids *paralleled* those of Hindu Brahmans. Nearly identical megalithic stone monuments "suddenly" sprang up throughout coastal Europe, the British isles, northern Africa, and the Pacific *long before* Phoenician sailors explored the seas, supposedly spreading such ideas and culture as they went. Stone-circle worship centers are almost identical no matter where in the world they are found, from England to Peru, from Polynesia to the State of Wyoming. What seemed to be the birth of the Golden Age of Reason around 500 B.C. (when Buddha, Pythagoras, Confucius, and Lao-tzu lived, and the secular use of runes began) was actually *a spontaneous global rediscovery and re-definition of ancient knowledge.*

As if these puzzles were not enough to think about, here are a few more. Names and games are almost identical throughout the world. Children's stories are equally similar, with over three-hundred versions of "Cinderella" known to exist. There is the Kalevala, a Finnish compilation of ancient mystical folk tales concerning creation, chivalry, heroism, and common life (more poetic and musical—right-brain-oriented); and there is the Kabbala, a Jewish compilation of ancient mystical interpretations of scripture emphasizing the nearness of God, secrets of creation, and the path to spiritual transformation (more detailed and linear—left-brain-oriented) ... one reflects the other in amazing ways. The Tree of Life is central to each, as is the message of God's importance in daily living. Interestingly, the Tree of Life is central to numerous spiritual and religious teachings and was in use as a sacred symbol *long before* the coming of Christianity *or* Judaism.

How did all this happen? By accident? Did UFOs zoom around seeding people's minds? Or did early humans understand flight and have airborne craft?

Although some evidence exists indicating the possibility of intergalactic visitors and ancient airplanes, it is usually not taken seriously. Most people simply label these happenings "coincidence" or assert that similar problems are solved by similar solutions. Neither idea, however, adequately addresses the amazing scope and consistency of plagiarism and cultural copying which was and still is rampant worldwide.

Even Indiana Jones, hero of the modern movie favorite *Raiders of the Lost Ark,* seems to be a hyped-up version of another adventurous archaeologist, Inigo Jones, who in the 1600s was commissioned by King Charles I of England to probe the mysteries of Stonehenge. Any invention you can name was invented at approximately the same time by a number of different people, each working independently and often unaware of the others' work. Invention credits have always been decided by who received recognition first, *rather than who invented first.* Magazine editors almost routinely deal with *spontaneous* repetitive submissions on the same subject, even if it is fiction. Unintentional copying occurs in every creative medium from music to math.

An old adage addresses this fact by stating, "Once it is done by one, it is done for all."

Sheldrake continues his theory by explaining that M-fields evolve. They are not static. Indeed, *no* layer of *any* kind of memory is static. Every thought, word, and deed, everything seen, heard, felt, or sensed, is stored away in some kind of memory storage bank, and each contribution to that storage bank either expands or diminishes the accumulated inventory. These invisible, floating "libraries" are accessible through the subconscious during moments of passive relaxation, intense concentration, or accelerated activity. We often enter and exit a full range of such "libraries" when we play, dream, imagine, wonder, muse, intuit, invent, experiment, read, reflect, meditate, create, compete, fantasize, focus, study, exercise, trance out, and so forth. Whenever we completely lose ourselves in what we are doing, whenever we focus or unfocus to the degree that all extraneous elements disappear, we automatically access memory fields and the depths of mass mind. We can alter or change whatever we find there.

Plato said, "All knowledge is recollection," implying that we learn only what we already know, are predisposed to, or are in harmony with.

Science tells us that it takes only one-tenth of one percent of a group of light waves to influence all the other light waves to follow them and create a pattern of coherence. If you swing one suspended steel beam in a room full of steel beams, soon all of them will be swinging in unison with the first. Women living together eventually experience their menses at the same time. Public trends in the marketplace and on Wall Street follow similar patterns. Is the threshold ratio of light waves also the threshold ratio for Sheldrake's M-fields, the human body, the collective mind and, for that matter, the varied forms of intelligence and matter itself?

Considering that science also tells us that matter is simply solidified light, we might reconsider the concept of resonance. Resonance is a stable condition caused by correlations between rhythm and coherence (the synchronicity of relationships in motion). It is a vibrating (oscillating) field array that forms and adheres to an overall pattern. This might account for the way memories work, for how one mind can affect all minds, and for how history—all history—is "remembered."

Receptivity, real magic, enables one to resonate with higher or different octaves of vibration. Thus, one can cohere (stick together or align with) patterns of energy. This is how rune casting works. We get in the mood by becoming receptive. When that happens, we begin to resonate and entrain with a broader version of the Greater Reality—and with layers upon layers of memory.

Simon Henderson, writing in the Fall 1987 issue of *Wildfire* magazine notes that there are two kinds of learning: symbol and pattern. He says individuals in pattern-literate societies have highly accurate recall of a vast array of knowledge, whereas individuals in symbol-literate societies require massive and elaborate materials storage—such as books, computers, libraries, and files. Symbol learning utilizes character representations like letters and numbers, while pattern learning utilizes muscle memory and harmonic memory.

Pattern knowledge that was passed on from one generation to the next is known as muscle memory (in dance) and harmonic memory (in song)—both of which are highly accurate in time. The sun verse of the Anasazi, for instance, was sung to a .001 second's accuracy each time, which is more accurate than most stopwatches. The time was remembered in their muscle movement and it was remembered in the song—and those that forgot could be reminded by others of the tribe, as all people shared this knowledge. The harmonic memory was also inherent in the art, which was not art as we understand it, but a sophisticated, scientific record of the common knowledge to which thousands of generations of people had added and amended information as new knowledge evolved.

There are West African tribes utilizing pattern oral knowledge in Nigeria who can chant back the combined knowledge of 1,600 to 2,000 generations, which traces back much further than the Bible. Traditional people in isolated islands in the South Pacific can still accurately navigate to over 1,500 islands using the same navigational patterns taught them by their ancestors.

Henderson went on to point out:

In contrasting the strengths of pattern-literate societies with our contemporary society we see that we produce individuals with university degrees who remember relatively little of what they have learned. Our civilization, rather than sharing in common knowledge, has produced such a wide diversity of specialized knowledge that we often feel isolated from one another.[26]

The basis of Henderson's ideas are similar to the writings of Jean M. Auel in her Earth Children Series.[27] Using the time frame of 35000 to 20000 B.C., she weaves a compelling story of one woman's life during that period, based on today's latest research. She also vividly describes the dream worlds of these early people, and the importance of collective memories as a major source of information, knowledge, and truth.

The dream concept Auel advances is not that different from the dreamtime concept of the Australian aborigines. The aborigines believe that two worlds exist, not just one: wake time and dreamtime. Each of these worlds is equally solid, real, active, and dynamic. According to the aboriginal belief, dreamtime can be entered in a number of ways: while asleep, by conscious will, through merging and joining, or because of a trance induced by sound, movement, or ingested substances. Once entered, dreamtime is said to operate slightly in advance of wake time, thus allowing "second sight" and the ability to become one with any person, place, or thing. Aborigines engaged in "dreaming" (the act of transferring consciousness from wake time to dreamtime) are renowned for their ability to "see" hundreds and sometimes thousands of miles away and to accurately report not only what they observe but also what they hear, feel, and smell. They prophesy in this state, and psychically intercede in cases where assistance can be given. The knowledge they gain from their version of dreaming is phenomenal in its precise and verifiable detail. Using modern terminology, it could be said that their beliefs actually describe two separate but parallel time/space continua, with one flowing somewhat ahead of the other. Random travel between these worlds is common, but specific journeys can be directed by conscious control.

The kind of memory reached from the depths of dreams is primordial in power and strength, yet we relegate it to symbolic myth in "civilized" society. Aboriginal dreaming is little different, really, from any other type of mind or spirit projection used by native peoples. What is often mistakenly classified as uncivilized or pagan behavior can actually be based on inner guidance and an acknowledgment of the sacredness and validity of memory.

If we are ever to understand the roots of our own being, we must first come to recognize that the psychic reality of dream life is as valid and important as the physical reality of waking existence.

Dreams and visions are the playground of the subconscious and a springboard to layers of memory. They are pathways to unlimited reserves of information and wisdom. You don't have to be asleep to experience them, nor is their content always relegated to the past.

By moving in and through dream depths, *consciously or subconsciously,* we can glimpse ancient memories of how images were formed and patterns took shape, of how behaviors were repeated into habits, and of how survival needs became so powerful that we have yet to satisfy them today, tens of thousands of years later. We meet our own beginnings in this memory dream-pool, our accumulated histories and possible futures, plus the reasons behind almost everything we do. All pathways sooner or later lead into this never-never land of the mind, so universal yet so intimate and personal. It is the doorway to our Source.

We are each the summation of countless millennia and untold rebirthings. Life does not so much graduate its members as it celebrates with them the continual rise of new beginnings.

No one can possess universal mind. It can be accessed by all but belongs to none. The only temporal claim we can make is to that small portion that is filtered and enhanced through our individual brains. Mind itself remains forever elusive and mysterious, even on the edge of the twenty-first century, but mind can be traveled and it can be used. We can harness endless potential from the limitless range of its power.

One mind, many thinkers.

Because there is only one mind, each of us has a vested interest in the existence and growth of all other forms of beingness. We are connected—you, I, all living things, and every level of intelligence. What happens to one of us somehow affects all of us, just as "the trembling of a daisy touches the farthest star."

Some people say that reincarnational memories surface when one begins to practice The Way of A Cast. Perhaps so. Yet to a surprising degree, anyone can "remember" runes. Certainly many of us have been personally affected by runes during our various sojourns (lifetimes) on earth, but nearly two decades of teaching runic secrets to others have convinced me that the childlike simplicity of the glyphs is what allows the collective mind to be tapped by anyone who wishes to do so.

The art of divination enables us to stop time, isolate a given moment, study its characteristics, discover its potential, and then compare our findings with their precedent from the realms of memory. This process takes only an instant, because an instant is the only time we really have.

History is cyclic. Civilizations come and go. Humankind learns and evolves and grows. But the mind continually encompasses and envelops all that exists, as if the mind were somehow an entity of its own ... pure consciousness aware of itself.

As our contemporary space travelers have proved that there are no boundaries upon the earth, so our creative spirit travelers have shown us that there are no boundaries within the mind.

CHAPTER EIGHT

Spirit Speaks

Songs and stories refer to runes as *lays* (short poems of deep feeling that are sung) and as *vignettes* (short stories filled with mystical mysteries that evoke emotional response). Artisans refer to runes as the ability to fashion pebblelike shapes into smooth mounds with rough, angular markings for the making of dishes. Lore masters refer to runes as powers for spell making and for healing wounds and illness.

It is clear that throughout history runes have signified more than a system of divination or of record keeping. Runes, *real* runes, seem to mean more than we think.

Indeed, long before there was ever a need for hieroglyphic script, there must have been a desire and a passion for re-creating patterns in the mind that would evoke the immediacy of special moments. These special moments would have been no less than ones where earth and sky, heaven and human, seemed to merge, intermingling the invisible with the visible. Such would have been times of awe and wonder . . . when spirit reigned.

These patterns in the mind would have quickly become anchored in collective memory because of their connection to basic comprehension levels and survival urges. Once fixed in memory, they would have become instinctual, and our response to them emotional.

These patterns in the mind are the real runes.

Runes are not just any type of sensory thought pattern. They are unique arrangements of shape and form that show us what to reach for and what to reject in our lives and in our environment. They are like subliminal survival symbols so powerfully entrenched within us that they seem to live and breathe with a life of their own.

Feeling joins with thought in rune use; the yin and the yang reunite.

Thus, real runes are the purest of magic and mystery. Once aroused or stimulated, they bring to your attention emotional responses suspended in time, responses connected to nature and everything that is natural. Real runes are affairs of the heart and messengers of the soul. We know them. We cannot forget them. No one can. They are too deeply embedded within our depths. We know them on a gut level, not a thinking level. We respond to them without knowing why. We understand them without any sense of logic. No one can honestly learn of runes, because none of us ever forgot them in the first place.

They strum the chords of our deepest memories. They are the "kisses" that life gives itself.

To regard runes only as glyphs graven on objects is to lose forever their true meaning. Glyphs are but representative designs . . . runes are living passion!

Of the many people who have written about runes, I know of only one individual in our technological age who even came close to stroking their secrets. Using the format of vignettes, he delved as deep as words can delve into the heart and soul of runes. His name was Sigurd F. Olson, and he was well known in his time as an avid ecologist and interpretive naturalist who dedicated his life to the understanding and preservation of wilderness. Sigurd was well educated, a professor and a dean, the recipient of many awards and honorary degrees, a past president of the Wilderness Society and National Parks Association, as well as a consultant to the U.S. Department of the Interior. He left this life in 1982, departing from his home in Ely, Minne-

sota, gateway to the wilds he came to know so well as a guide
in his youth.

Olson was familiar with the Kalevala and understood its runic
lays. He knew Nordic and Finnish history and the myths of old.
Among his many books was the simple yet eloquent *Runes of
the North*. Its publisher, Alfred A. Knopf, has granted me permission to quote some passages. These brief glimpses will at
least give you a "taste" and "feel" for what I believe runes
really are.

Tall aspen stand among the cedars surrounding the cabin,
and as the wind blows they whisper an ancient song.
Along the ridge protecting it from the north are birches
growing among the rocks, clusters of striped maple, and
hazel. Chickadees and nuthatches are around my sauna
cabin, and in one of the tallest trees, pileated woodpeckers
have built their nest.

A flying squirrel lives in a hole under the roof and,
when it comes out, it spreads its legs and sails to the
nearest balsam. I saw it the other night and its eyes were
liquid and black, its fur a greyish tan and softer than chin-
chilla, its wing strips edged with stable. A beautiful crea-
ture, I am glad it has taken its abode in so important a
place as my sauna.

Along the trail to the lake are huge stones with depressions between them reaching down to the dark, wet roots
of the cedar. The boulders are covered with sphagnum and
in it grow gold thread, violets, and strange fungi. All these
living things are part of the sauna cabin, as they are part
of the woods and rocks around it. It is a place of delight
and beauty woven into the experience itself.

Over the lake lay a sense of impending doom and we make everything safe: canoes well up among the trees, tent stakes reinforced, ropes so tight they sang when we touched them. All we owned was covered: food, equipment, dry wood under tarpaulins weighted down with heavy stones. We were at the shore ready to fly for the tent the instant the wind and deluge came.

Then a strange and eerie light was over the lake and the surrounding hills, a greenish-yellow glow that was almost tarnished gold. Rushes once black were illumined now, leaned like rapiers as the air began to move. The stump became alive, lost its jagged contours, and was a thing of beauty against the opalescence of the water. The cliffs and pines against the channel turned to burnished copper. Then came the wind and the rain in a final crashing rumble— and the glory was gone.

My little dream net spoke of many things to me, of love for children, of tolerance and the intangible qualities which give warmth and meaning to life. When I accepted it, I did so with humility because to me it was a symbol not only of trust and acceptance by my Indian friend, but a hint of the long past and a world of dreams most moderns have forgotten.

Not long ago, I slept under a pine tree with my six-year-old grandson Derek. We had a tiny fire and lay in our sleeping bags watching the reflection of dying embers against the branches and how it turned them to gold and bronze and copper. I told him many stories of moose and bear and, at the end, the legend of the dream net; he believed, for he was young and still had faith. Above us that night was the ancient net, and the night was full of dreams both good and bad. He could see them, feel them, and when I told him that only the good ones came through, he closed his eyes quietly and went to sleep.[28]

If you have never read *Runes of the North* by Sigurd F. Olson, do so, for it is a treasure. The book has been reprinted numerous times, and is available through most libraries.

Olson writes as near as anyone can of real runes, those sensorial patterns in the mind formed by our emotional response to moments uniquely memorable, yet common to us all. These runes, true runes, are beyond the reach of words . . . for they are *the language the pure essence of spirit speaks.*

Spirit speaks through The Way of A Cast, coaxing us ever so gently to step into our dreams, so we can recognize that the dreamer and the dream and the soul of all dreams are one and the same.

Spirit speaks in the heart tugs we have when Goddess Runes unite the mystery of creation with the miracle of life, so we can reconnect with The Source of *All* Being.

Spirit speaks to each of us—when we listen.

CHAPTER NINE

Woman Speaks

Rune casting has been part of my life's journey. Goddess Runes and The Way of A Cast were introduced to me when I was newly recovered from devastating health traumas and three encounters with The Other Side. As I became acquainted with the feminine aspects of the runes, I became reacquainted with myself as the woman I am.

Making peace with my own femininity necessitated that I explore my past and search out those areas where gender issues had been a problem. It didn't take long for these to surface. Let me share some of them with you.

I was sexually molested by an uncle at the age of four and was threatened with dire consequences should I ever tell. Determined that men like my uncle would never have power over me again, I started identifying more with the masculine gender, became a tomboy, and immersed myself in topics like economics, business, and the sciences. "Anything for Adventure" became my motto; anything feminine I avoided, for it represented weakness to me. My family had other plans for my life, however. My mother made it clear that I had to learn how to work hard, sacrifice much, and accept the pain of "a woman's role." My father firmly stated that college was out of the question: "The only reason a girl goes to college is to find a man. Find yours here; it's cheaper." I did what my parents requested.

Society reflected back to me what I had learned growing up. For example, in the fifties, the man who employed me said to my face that I could never be paid the same wages as a man simply because I was a woman, even though I worked the same job—and did the work better. In the sixties, I literally had doors slammed in my face because I dared to apply for store-management positions that were reserved for male applicants only. In the seventies, I was advised that the world was not ready yet for female bank executives or money brokers. In the eighties, I was severely criticized at times because I, a mere near-death survivor and a woman to boot, had the audacity to go out and do my own independent research on the near-death phenomenon and publish a book about my findings. (My publisher in Holland, a firm founded by a man who used three initials as his forename, changed my name on the book's cover without my knowledge or permission because "women can't have three initials for a name." He never asked, but I would have told him if he had that my "strange" name came to me in a vision I hold sacred, and as such is my legal and full name.)

As I learned about the nuances and subtleties of Goddess Runes, I came to view my role as a woman differently. Grace of posture and speech is a byproduct of using this runic system, as is a more gentle demeanor. Whether male or female, one is led to a sense of community and responsible interactions. The deeper I delved into rune lore, the better I felt about myself in particular, and male and female issues in general. I could see, through the evolution of the runic designs, that sexual energies, regardless of what role anyone plays, are complementary forces meant to nurture and enhance—not divide and conquer. The issue has never been one of gender, but of politics and power.

We have been taught, collectively, that the female is inferior, the male superior. This idea of inferior/superior grew out of the subordination of women, when overzealous political and religious movements established class systems to protect property ownership, which included slavery. "Power over" (domination) replaced "power to" (individual rights). Since historians have almost exclusively been men, they recorded what men did. Yet there has never been a dearth of heroines, just men with short memories.

Women have always been incredible leaders and have accomplished great deeds; take, for instance, Hildegard of the Rhineland. She was a poet, scholar, and mystic, who used her abilities to challenge both ecclesiastical and civil governments and force change and reform. She was a pioneer in science, wrote two treatises on various aspects of medicine and natural history, and, for recreation, contrived her own language. She traveled extensively throughout Europe as an outspoken critic, and conducted lengthy correspondences with four popes, two emperors, and Henry II of England. Although never formally canonized after her death in 1179, she was proclaimed a saint by the many people who credited miracles to her. Hildegard's vigor and her vision are still inspiring, even on the edge of the twenty-first century.[29]

Two women have come forward lately with books that give unusual insight into what happens to women when faced with the inferior/superior bias, and how they can be healed. They are Clarissa Pinkola Estés and Naomi Ruth Lowinsky, both professional therapists and storytellers.

Estés, in *Women Who Run With the Wolves*, speaks of the Wild Woman archetype, that deeply instinctual psyche in all females, that desire to be natural, to sing with the soul voice the song of life and death, of creation's story.[30] In an interview conducted by Peggy Taylor and printed in the November/December 1992 issue of *New Age Journal,* Estés is quoted as saying:

The Wild Woman archetype has to do with the ability to discern what is needed in both our inner and outer lives at any given moment. It is the aspect of women's psyches that knows. It knows, it knows, and it knows, and no matter what you do to a woman, it still knows. She may be distanced from that voice—which I would call the voice of the ''soul-Self''—but eventually, and most likely through her suffering, she will be brought back to that center. She will begin by hook or by crook to listen again to what it says to her, because it broadcasts to her what she should do next, what is in her interest, what she should beware of. The wildish instinctual nature not only strengthens her but also, through breathtaking intuitions, insights, images, and thoughts, gives her explicit maps and instructions.[31]

Lowinsky helps us to reevaluate the generational roles of women in her book, *Stories from the Motherline: Reclaiming the Mother-Daughter Bond, Finding Our Feminine Souls* (recently renamed *The Motherline: Everywoman's Journey to Find Her Female Roots*).[32] Lowinsky has been gracious in allowing me to quote at random from an article she wrote about "Grandmother Consciousness" (featured in the September/October 1990 issue of *New Realities* magazine, a publication no longer printed).

A grandmother locates an individual in the life stream of the generations. She is the tie to the subterranean world of the female ancestors. When three generations of women are together, a sacred trinity is evoked: the three ages of woman, the three aspects of the goddess—Maiden, Mother, Crone—which have been worshipped in many cultures since the earliest ages . . .

The grandmother has access to the objectivity of the Feminine. One generation removed from the heat and passion, she can see with the cold eye of the witch, with the irreverent eye of the gossip, with the healing vision of the wise woman . . .

As the fourth generation emerges, as the three become four, the feminine self experiences the wholeness of continuity. Integrated grandmother consciousness can hold the opposites of being involved and distant, of embodying the motherline and not embodying it. This is the larger perspective she can bring to her granddaughter: standing behind her and before her, opening doors to the deeper

chambers of the Feminine, that little-known place in our
culture where birth and death, body and soul, are kin, and
where lives loop through time as through the figure eight
of infinity, always changing, always the same.

As a brief aside, Lowinsky reminds us that the word "gossip" originally meant "god speaking through a woman," and
referred to a woman who is a godparent or a member of the
congregation of women at a childbirth. Telling stories from the
motherline, literally, is gossiping.

I challenge all females to discover the wild woman and the
motherline within themselves and in their own lives. We each
are the maiden, the mother, the crone. We each are the hearth
keeper and the wise woman and the wildish witch. We each
are the singers of creation's story, for whether we give birth or
not, we pass on our blood and the soft touch of our love.

While many people today remind us of the power of goddess
energy, some of the most eloquent are men who have rediscovered their own feminine qualities, such as Sam Keen, who
writes of recapturing the sacred in everything we do everyday
of our lives. His book, *Hymns to an Unknown God: Awakening
the Spirit in Everyday Life,*[33] is a treasure of thoughtful
reflections.

Gender bias isn't so much men against women, to my way
of thinking, as it is society itself coming to grips with its own
self-serving refusal to acknowledge the value of inner wisdom
and knowing (gnosis). We've relegated subjectivity and intuition to females, when that necessary balance to objective logic
potentially exists in everyone, regardless of gender.

No, gender bias is not males versus females. It is the clash
of control versus sharing, domination versus freedom, acquired
knowledge versus spontaneous knowing, of a head that has lost
its heart.

The age of law and the age of faith are now in decline. A
new age is aborning—the age of personal experience—where
the head reunites with the heart, the male with the female. This
is the new magic, not only femininity reclaimed, but the whole

healed. That's our challenge, to bring together that which has been separated, to heal.

The "truthsense" of inner wisdom cannot be taught; it is *experienced* and *remembered.*

Casting honors the goddess, not because females have been the principal rune casters throughout the vast ages of time, but because casting leads an individual beyond stereotypes and archetypes into the depths of the soul. The skill achieved in doing this helps one to touch the pulse of life and its need to spin and grow. This enables one to breathe the authentic breath—aliveness.

My journey is all our journeys, for we are all learning how to claim our worth and our power without losing the kindness of caring for one another, without losing the guidance we need to find our way in a world no longer warmed by the friendly "fires" of respect and integrity.

May the pages you turned in reading this book return to your fingers the aliveness of your being. May the runes you cast reunite you with the greatness that you are.

Always look beyond
what you can see,
for the purpose
of truth
is
to extend
your view.

Resource Suggestions

Because I honor the divine right of each individual to pursue his or her own path toward The Truth of One's Being and the grace of an inspired life, my books always include a resource section. It is not my intention to present a comprehensive index, but rather, a gesture of sharing some of the best sources and resources currently available. I cannot make any promises or guarantees about anything listed here, but I can offer this section as a place to begin your own search for additional information. It is my hope that you will find this material interesting, helpful, and, above all, challenging.

Topics are arranged aphabetically as follows:

Addendum on Runes
Archaeology, Astro-Archaeology, Earth Energy, Ley Lines
Bau-Biologie
Devas, Nature Spirits, Angels
Dowsing
Dreams and Mythology
Feng Shui (Chinese Geomancy)
Goddess Energy Renewal
Huna
Intuition and The Psychic
Near-Death Experience

Reincarnation
Sounds and Language
Spirituality and Meditation
Storytelling
The Old Ways
The Work of P.M.H. Atwater, Lh.D.

ADDENDUM ON RUNES

You can find pebbles very much like the ones I have through various sources, among them gift shops, gemstone catalogs, flower-arranging boutiques, and some garden stores. Ask for **Japanese polished stones** used to anchor flower arrangements, or simply "stones by the pound." Many times you can find stores selling crystals and gemstones that are cut and tumbled to a perfect size for rune use. One garden catalog that carries the Japanese flower-arranging stones is Smith and Hawken Gardening Catalogue, 25 Corte Madera, Mill Valley, CA 94941; (415) 383-2000. A gift catalog that lists the right size of rose quartz and hematite can be obtained from The Nature Company, P.O. Box 2310, Berkeley, CA 94702; 1-800-227-1114. Naturally, if you can find your own stones out in the wilds, they will mean more to you, and they will be more personal.

A new way of using Futhark runes was developed by Joe Ann Van Gelder. Inspired by an angelic presence, Van Gelder created a system of working directly with the **energy pattern** of each yang rune for the purpose of healing and self-empowerment. With conscious transformation as the goal, she has put together a kit to aid those who might wish to take advantage of this process. Contact her through: Vermont Vibrations, 17 Memphremagog Views, Newport, VT 05855; (802) 334-2341.

There is a renaissance of poetry occurring today. Since poetry is so much a part of rune lore, I would encourage you to discover the work of Bill Moyers, both his book and the Public Broadcasting System televised documentary he hosted on the subject. Refer to *The Language of Life* by Bill Moyers (Doubleday, New York City, 1995), and to the eight-part documentary, same name, which began June 30, 1995.

ARCHAEOLOGY, ASTRO-ARCHAEOLOGY, EARTH ENERGY, LEY LINES

Paul Devereux is an expert in this field, and he is one of the people spearheading the Dragon Project in England, whereby exacting measurements are being made of ley lines (energy grids) and how they dissect ancient megalithic monuments. Devereux is the author of twelve books on this subject. Among them are *The New Ley Hunter's Companion, Earth Lights, Lines on the Landscape: Leys and Other Enigmas* (with Nigel Pennick), *Earthmind* (with John Steele and David Kubrin), and *Shamanism and the Mystery Lines.* Devereux edits and publishes *The Ley Hunter: The Magazine of Earth Mysteries,* which is outstanding. Through Devereux, you can obtain an important book about divinatory practices, *Games of the Gods: The Origin of Board Games in Magic and Divination,* by Nigel Pennick and published in England. Contact: Paul Devereux, P.O. Box 92, Penzance, Cornwall, TR18 2XL, England.

The Archaeological Conservancy is an organization dedicated to buying sacred sites for the purpose of ensuring their preservation. Considering the pace at which these sites are being torn down or destroyed, everyone's help is needed to stop the trend. Whether you have money to donate, ideas, or time to offer, contact them at 415 Orchard Drive, Santa Fe, NM 87501; (505) 982-3278.

Sig Lonegren runs an apprenticeship training program for the construction and proper use of sacred spaces. For the last twenty-five years, Lonegren has been working on ways to improve intuition while at the same time seeking equal input from the rational mind. He has found that intuition is increased by using tools like sacred space, dowsing, and labyrinths. He wrote *Spiritual Dowsing* and *Labyrinths: Ancient Myths & Mod-*

ern Uses, both published by Gothic Image Publications in London, England, and available in the U.S. Contact him directly concerning his apprenticeship program: Sig Lonegren, Box 218, Greensboro, VT 05841. Similar opportunities are offered in England through: OakDragan Project, P.O. Box 5, Castle Cary, Somerset BA7 7YQ, England.

OTHER BOOKS ON THE SUBJECT

Earth Energies: A Quest for the Hidden Power of the Planet, Serge Kahili King. Wheaton, IL; Quest Theosophical Publishing House, 1992.

The New View Over Atlantis, John Michel. New York, NY; Harper & Row, 1983.

Sacred Places: How the Living Earth Seeks Our Friendship, James Swan. Santa Fe, NM; Bear & Company, 1990

Sacred Sites: A Guidebook to Sacred Centers & Mysterious Places in the United States, edited by Frank Joseph. St. Paul, MN; Llewellyn Press, 1992.

The Stars and the Stones, Martin Brennan. London, England; Thames and Hudson, 1983.

BAU-BIOLOGIE

Bau-Biologie is the science of holistic interactions between life and environment. It came out of the concern for the effect of the environment on health. The comprehensive system addresses selection of proper building site, house design, energy aspects, heating/ventilation/air filtration, electrical installation, selection of proper building materials, light/illumination/color, furniture and interior design. Inquire about classes and practitioners in your area. Contact: International Institute For Bau-Biologie & Ecology, Inc., Box 387, Clearwater, FL 34615; (813) 461-4371.

DEVAS, NATURE SPIRITS, ANGELS

Currently referred to as **devas** (shining ones) and **nature spirits** (spirit helpers), the angels and fairies of lore are back, mostly because so many people in diverse areas have had such remarkable experiences working with them. Most successful have been gardeners and those concerned with ecology. Legendary in this area is the **Community of Findhorn**, located on the northeastern coast of Scotland. What began as an experiment to see how well humans could co-create with the spirit kingdom in growing vegetables and flowers became a showplace of spiritual law in action. Findhorn is extensive in scope. Contact: The Accommodation Secretary, Findhorn Foundation, Cluny Hill College, Forres 1V36 ORD, Scotland; Forres (0309) 72288.

OTHER BOOKS ON THE SUBJECT OF DEVAS AND
NATURE SPIRITS

Behaving As If the God in All Life Mattered and *The Perelandra Garden Workbook: A Complete Guide to Gardening with Nature Intelligences,* both by Machaelle Small Wright. Available through Perelandra, Ltd., Box 3603, Warrenton, VA 20188; 24-Hour Answering Phone (504) 937-2153.

The Magic of Findhorn, Paul Hawken. New York, NY; Harper & Row, 1975.

To Hear the Angels Sing: An Odyssey of Co-Creation with the Devic Kingdom, Dorothy Maclean (of Findhorn fame). Middletown, WI; Lorian Press, 1983.

SOME GOOD RESOURCES ON ANGELS

Angels: The Role of Celestial Guardians and Beings of Light, Paola Giovetti. York Beach, ME; Samuel Weiser, Inc., 1993.

The Angels Around Us, John Randolph Price. New York, NY; Ballantine Books (Fawcett Columbine), 1993.

Commune with the Angels: A Heavenly Handbook, Jane M. Howard. Virginia Beach, VA; A.R.E. Press, 1992.

Where Angels Walk: True Stories of Heavenly Visitors, a compilation by Joan Wester Anderson. New York, NY; Bantam Books, 1992.

The most articulate exponent of angel realms today is K. Martin-Kuri, an artist of world renown and a student of Rudolf Steiner's teachings. She has initiated national and international conferences on angels that have drawn together thousands in an exploration of how people can better prepare themselves to serve with angels. She has initiated unique classroom materials, and continues to showcase her stunning paintings. Her newest book, *A Message for the Millennium* (Ballantine Books, New York City, 1996), is of unusual quality. For more information, contact: 28-Angels, Inc., P.O. Box 116, Free Union, VA 22940; 1-800-28ANGEL.

DOWSING

Dowsing is the most constructive way I know to explore and expand intuitive/psychic abilities. And it is fun! Anyone from a four-year-old to great-grandparents can do it. Contrary to some notions, dowsing is not a "special gift" but is readily teachable as a practical skill to access octaves of vibration beyond the electromagnetic spectrum. **Dowsers are the doers of psi. The bottom line is always demonstration and results.** The two best books on the subject are:

The Divining Hand, Christopher Bird. Black Mountain, NC; New Age Press, 1985.

The Divining Mind, Edward Ross and Richard D. Wright. Rochester, VT; Destiny Books, 1990.

The American Society of Dowsers, Inc., is quite large, fully reputable, and sponsors an annual conference that is one of the finest events I have ever attended. Their *Journal* is excellent, and they offer a full line of books, equipment, and materials related to the subject of dowsing. Many local chapters of the organization sprinkled across the country hold regional conferences as well. Contact: The American Society of Dowsers, Inc., Box 24, Danville, VT 05828-0024; (802) 684-3417. You may contact their bookstore directly: ASD Bookstore, P.O. Box 4, Danville, VT 05828-0024; (802) 684-1176.

As a brief aside, **brain-mapping equipment was used in actual field tests** to determine what speed of brain waves a person registered who was involved in dowsing. Consistently, these tests showed that both the fastest brain-wave function (beta or wide awake) and the slowest (delta or deep sleep) predominated. This surprised the researchers, as they had expected a readout of strong alpha waves (equivalent to a drowsy state, neither awake nor asleep, when the average person is more receptive to psychic or creative promptings). Implied in this finding is that dowsing tends to synergize right- and left-brain hemispheres so individuals can become more whole-brained. Thus, the conscious mind and the subconscious mind can work together more closely or merge. It is my supposition that rune casting is similar to dowsing in how it affects brain-wave function.

DREAMS AND MYTHOLOGY

ON DREAMS

The Dream Dictionary, Jo Jean Boushahla and Virginia Reidel-Geubtner. New York, NY; Pilgrim, 1983.

Getting Help from Your Dreams, Henry Reed. Virginia Beach, VA: Inner Vision Publishing Company, 1985.

How to Interpret Your Dreams: An Encyclopedic Dictionary, Tom Chetwynd. New York, NY; P.H. Wyden, 1980.

The Inner Eye: Your Dreams Can Make You Psychic, Joan Windsor. Englewood Cliffs, NJ; Prentice-Hall, 1985.

Lucid Dreaming: The Power of Being Awake and Aware in Your Dreams, Stephen LaBerge, Ph.D. Los Angeles, CA: J.P. Tarcher, 1985.

Our Dreaming Mind, Robert L. Van de Castle, Ph.D. New York, NY; Ballantine Books, 1994.

Personal Mythology: The Psychology of Your Evolving Self: Using Ritual, Dreams, and Imagination to Discover Your Inner Story, David Feinstein, Ph.D., and Stanley Krippner, Ph.D. Los Angeles, CA: J.P. Tarcher, 1988.

ON MYTHOLOGY

The Hero with a Thousand Faces, Joseph Campbell. New York, NY; Princeton University Press (Bollingen Series 27), 1973.

Heroes of the Kalevala, Finland's Saga, Babette Deutsch. New York, NY; Julian Messner (Pocket Books), 1966.

The Global Myths: Exploring Primitive, Pagan, Sacred, and Scientific Mythologies, Alexander Eliot. New York, NY; Truman Talley Books/Meridian, 1994.

Kansanruno-Kalevala, Elias Lonnrot, edited by Matti Kuusi. Keuruu, Finland; Otava Publishing Co., 1977.

The Larousse Encyclopedia of Mythology, translated by Richard Aldrington and Delano Ames. New York, NY; Barnes and Noble Books, 1994.

Memories and Visions of Paradise: Exploring the Universal Myth of a Lost Golden Age, Richard Heinberg. Los Angeles, CA; J.P. Tarcher, 1989.

Poems of the Elder Edda, translation by Patricia Terry. Philadelphia, PA; University of Pennsylvania Press, 1990.

The Power of Myth, Joseph Campbell with Bill Moyers. New York, NY; Doubleday, 1988. This book is a summary of the PBS television series. Moyers interviewed Campbell, the world's foremost authority on myths, on the power and purpose of mythology. The series was so compelling that it has become six one-hour videos plus an audiocassette program. Check your local bookstores.

The Secret Teachings of All Ages, Manley P. Hall. Originally published in 1928 by the Philosophical Research Society of Los Angeles, CA. Reprinted by them in 1978 and still available.

For more information about **the Kalevala and other folklore,** inquire through The American Folklife Center, Library of Congress, Washington, D.C. 20540-8100; (202) 707-6590.

There is **a magazine that specializes in magic, myth, and fantasy.** For everything from the latest Arthurian sagas to the newest heroic quests, from ancient myths to contemporary interviews and articles, *Realms of Fantasy* has it all. To obtain a copy or subscribe, write: *Realms of Fantasy,* P.O. Box 736, Mt. Morris, IL 61054.

FENG SHUI (CHINESE GEOMANCY)

Feng Shui (Chinese geomancy) is the art of living in harmony with the land and deriving the greatest benefit, peace, and prosperity from being in the right place at the right time. It has two schools or systems of practice—the intuitive and the analytical. Easy or complicated, depending on which method you use, Feng Shui can be immensely practical. It can aid you in building your home in proper balance with the land it sits upon, remodeling what you already have into proper order, or planning your rooms, decor, and usage of available space. Some books on the subject:

Feng Shui: The Chinese Art of Designing a Harmonious Environment, Derek Walters. New York, NY; Simon and Schuster, 1988.

Feng Shui: The Chinese Art of Placement, Sarah Rossbach. New York, NY; E.P. Dutton, 1983.

Interior Design with Feng Shui, Sarah Rossbach. New York, NY; E.P. Dutton, 1987.

The Living Earth Manual of Feng Shui, Stephen Skinner. London, England; Routledge & Kegan Paul, 1982.

Feng Shui is helpful for restructuring what is already built by correlating buildings to the earth's natural energy flow. This flow is called "dragon currents," or "chi," and compares favorably with east/west energy movements of the earth-pulse at about seven hertz. Thus, Feng Shui utilizes north/south orientations to harness and redirect chi. Compasses were built to measure all aspects of this energy and assist with building construction. For this reason, Feng Shui is the progenitor of modern magnetic compasses, navigation, and geography. Other sources of information:

American School of Geomancy, P.O. Box 1039, Sebastopol, CA 95473-1039; (707) 829-8413. Featuring the work of Richard Feather Anderson, this school teaches the Americanized version of Feng Shui. Comprehensive experiential programs are provided for in-depth training in the principles and practice of "the art of enhancing sense of place and well-being and living in harmony with the earth's patterns." Intuition and sacred geometry are central to this system.

Sweet Fern Magazine, Route #1, Box 566, Walpole, NH 03608; (603) 756-4152. Featuring the work of Bob and Celeste Longacre, this small publication is a treasure trove of right living and right placement suggestions and techniques. Bob Longacre combines many different disciplines into his own unique version of ecologically sound environmental systems. Offers workshops, classes, and slide shows. Travels as well as publishes.

GODDESS ENERGY RENEWAL

An Anthology of Sacred Texts by and About Women, edited by Serinity Young. New York, NY; The Crossroad Publishing Company, 1993.

Ancient Mirrors of Womanhood: A Treasury of Goddess and Heroine Lore from Around the World, Merlin Stone. Boston, MA; Beacon Press, 1979.

The Chalice and the Blade: Our History, Our Future, Riane Eisler. San Francisco, CA: Harper & Row, 1988.

Dancing Up the Moon: A Woman's Guide to Creating Traditions That Bring Sacredness to Daily Life, Robin Heerens Lysne. San Bernardino, CA; Borgo Press, 1995.

The Fear of the Feminine and Other Essays on Feminine Psychology, Erich Neumann. Princeton, NJ; Princeton University Press, 1994.

Feminine Face of God: The Unfolding of the Sacred in Women, Sherry Anderson and Patricia Hopkins. New York, NY; Bantam Books, 1991.

Goddesses in Everywoman: A New Psychology of Women, Jean S. Bolen. San Francisco, CA; Harper & Row, 1984. And its companion volume, *Gods in Everyman: A New Psychology of Men's Lives & Loves,* Jean Shinoda Bolen. San Francisco, CA; Harper & Row, 1989.

Goddess in the Office, Zsuzsanna Budapest. San Francisco, CA: Harper San Francisco, 1992.

Grandmothers of the Light: A Medicine Woman's Source Book, Paula Gunn Allen. Boston, MA; Beacon Press, 1991.

In the Wake of the Goddess: Women, Culture, and the Biblical Transformation of Pagan Myth, Tikva Frymer-Kensky. New York, NY; Free Press, 1991.

Megatrends for Women, Patricia Aburdene & John Naisbitt. New York, NY; Villard Books, 1992.

The Once and Future Goddess: A Symbol for Our Time, Elinor Gadon. San Francisco, CA; Harper & Row, 1989.

When God Was a Woman, Merlin Stone. San Diego, CA; Harcourt, Brace, Jovanovich, 1976.

Wise Women of the Dreamtime, Aboriginal Tales of the Ancestral Power (no author listed). Rochester, VT; Inner Traditions, 1992.

The Woman's Encyclopedia of Myths and Secrets, Barbara Walker. San Francisco, CA; Harper & Row, 1983.

The 13 Original Clan Mothers, Jamie Sams. San Francisco, CA; Harper/SanFrancisco, 1993.

HERBALS FOR WOMEN'S HEALTH

Healing Wise and *Childbearing Years* and *Menopausal Years*—all by Susun S. Weed, and available through Ash Tree Publishing, P.O. Box 64, Woodstock, NY 12498.

Herbal Ways for Women: Natural Remedies for All the Phases of a Woman's Life and Health, Rosemary Gladstar. New York, NY; Simon and Schuster, 1993.

TWO IMPORTANT VIDEOS

Goddess Remembered (explores the values, art, architecture, and traditions of cultures where women played an equal or leading role); and *Burning Times* (looks at the Inquisition, that three-hundred-year period beginning in the thirteenth century when the Catholic Church tortured and murdered hundreds of thousands, possibly millions, of people—the majority of whom were women involved in traditional or goddess-oriented religions, midwifery, and home healing). Both of these outstanding videos are available through Direct Cinema Ltd., Box 69799, Los Angeles, CA 90069-9976.

CELEBRATING RITES OF PASSAGE

Donna Henes, author of *Celestially Auspicious Occasions, Seasons, Cycles and Celebrations* (Putnam, New York City, 1995). She is active in sponsoring special events and rites of passage, and in giving classes. Contact her for more information or to reserve space at one of her events: Donna Henes, P.O. Box 380403, Brooklyn, NY 11238-0403; (718) 857-2247.

D. Layne Humphrey, 4360 Mary Ridge Drive, Randallstown, MD 21133; (410) 655-1334. Humphrey is one of a growing number who are offering training for women who wish to learn how to celebrate the major phases in a woman's life, such as entering puberty, the menstrual matrix, reclaiming the wise woman, menopause. If you are unable to take advantage of the classes, workshops, and retreats Humphrey offers, look for similar opportunities in your own area or start such group-work yourself.

HUNA

The best way I know to introduce you to this philosophical yet practical religion of the Hawaiian Islands is through the organization called **Huna Research, Inc.** Founded in 1945 by Max Freedom Long and currently directed by E. Otha Wingo, Ph.D., it is dedicated to the preservation, dissemination, and offering of Huna writings, materials, teaching tools, and classes. Kahunas, those who practiced Huna, were incredible healers and advanced one of the most effective forms of psychology and interpersonal group dynamics I have yet seen. For more information, contact: Huna Research, Inc., 1760 Anna Street, Cape Girardeau, MO 63701; (573) 334-3478.

INTUITION AND THE PSYCHIC

Logic and Intutition are equal partners. Without both working together harmoniously, we are neither healthy nor balanced. Logic, a product of conscious and deliberate thought, is considered a left-brain activity. Intuition, a product of subconscious abstractions, is most often associated with the right hemisphere of the brain. There has been ample scientific research now to prove the wisdom of **right-brain development** and the folly of exclusive dependence on left-brain linear thinking. A healthy brain is a whole brain, in which all parts work together effectively and equally.

As we expand our creative and intuitive potential, we develop solid, dependable skills and abilities with which to explore our inner life and dreamscapes. A question to ask is: how can we ever reach and endure transcended states of consciousness until we can first learn to utilize and integrate the inner realities of our own mind? Visualization and dream interpretation are positive, safe ways to begin.

The dynamics of inner realities are really the same thing as psychic abilities. The only difference is one of semantics. **The psychic and the intuitive are the same.** Psychic powers are simply extensions of natural sensing faculties normal to us. It is all a matter of usage and purpose. Perhaps the best way to think of this and keep everything in a healthy perspective is to concentrate on developing ourselves to be the best we can, to emphasize virtue, responsibility, joy, and service. All else will assume its rightful proportions if we do.

Psychic ability developed just for its own sake will backfire. Notice, for instance, how many psychics lead miserable lives and/or drink excessively, smoke heavily, or are hooked on drugs and sex. **Being "accurate" is not necessarily a sign of competence.** Psychic abilities developed out of context from our practical and spiritual natures represent the negative aspects of inner growth, in my opinion. But psychic abilities developed as part of a balanced, wholesome life are invaluable. Skills of the inner life are just as valid and desirable as skills of the outer life. Anything you can already do, you can always learn to do better.

The best long-established organization which serves as a guidepost for the sane, constructive exploration of psychism as it relates to wholesome, spiritual development, is the **Association for Research and Enlightenment** (A.R.E.). Highly diversified, they offer a complete range of books, tapes, class-and-seminar opportunities, therapeutic health departments, a health clinic, a list of cooperating doctors, summer camps, study groups throughout the world, library facilities, the Atlantic University for the study of consciousness, ongoing research projects, and much, much more. Their magazine, *Venture Inward,* is truly remarkable. Introductory packets with book catalogs are free for the asking. Contact: A.R.E., P.O. Box 595, Virginia Beach, VA 23451; 1-800-333-4499. (To call their bookstore, dial 1-800-723-1112.) By the way, the A.R.E. has just created a "Psychic Training Mentor Program" for anyone who wishes to develop or improve his or her psychic ability. This is a five-level training track headed by Carol Ann Liaros and Henry Reed, Ph.D. Be certain to inquire about it.

Another reliable organization, which is more of a movement than a fixed-base operation, is **Spiritual Frontiers Fellowship** (S.F.F.). Although they don't offer the same programs for beginners, they do have a challenging and stimulating summertime retreat program at various college campuses across the country. Attracting some of the finest talent in the field, their retreats are lively and enjoyable as well as diverse. Their quarterly *Journal* is excellent. Spiritual Frontiers Fellowship also maintains a library, local study groups, and various educational programs. Queries are welcome. Contact: S.F.F., P.O. Box 7868, Philadelphia, PA 19109; (215) 222-1991.

Although not as large or diverse as the two previous organizations, **Spiritual Advisory Council** (S.A.C.) deserves to be mentioned here. In existence for over fifteen years, the organization has established itself as a source of outstanding summertime seminars held in various locations, plus classes and ministerial training for the purpose of teaching the spiritual use of psychic abilities. National and international speakers are often featured. Queries are welcome. Contact: S.A.C., 14345 S.E. 103rd Terrace, Summerfield, FL 34491; (352) 288-6607.

The purpose of Global Intuition Network (G.I.N.) is to promote the applied use of intuition in decision making, to share new knowledge on how to use this skill as it becomes known, and to promote ongoing research on intuitive processes for practical use in organizations and business. Initiated by Weston Agor, Ph.D., the network expands on ideas first introduced in Agor's challenging book: *Intuition in Organizations—Leading and Managing Productively* (Sage Publications, Newbury Park, CA; 1989). International support and participation has mushroomed since G.I.N. began, making the network an important resource for the practical development and use of intuition as a skills-enhancement tool. For information about their international conferences and membership, contact: G.I.N., The University of Texas at El Paso, El Paso, TX 79968-0614; (915) 747-5227.

Four of the most constructive and practical manuals for psychic development may not be available in bookstores. Contact directly:

Develop Your Psychic Skills (and *Expand Your Psychic Skills*), Enid Hoffman. West Chester, PA; Para Research, Inc., various years depending on edition.

Harold Sherman's Great ESP Manual, Mrs. Harold Sherman, HC 74, Box 232, Highway 5 South, Mountain View, AR 72560.

Natural ESP: A Layman's Guide to Unlocking the Extra Sensory Power of Your Mind, Ingo Swann. New York, NY; Bantam Books, 1987.

*Practical ESP: A Step By Step Guide for Developing Your Intu-
itive Potential,* Carol Ann Liaros, Blind Awareness Project,
1966 Niagara Street, Suite 101, Buffalo, NY 14207.

BOOKS TO BROADEN YOUR UNDERSTANDING OF
PSYCHISM—ADULTS

*Conscious Evolution: Understanding Extrasensory Abilities in
Everyday Life,* Janet Lee Mitchell, Ph.D. New York, NY;
Ballantine Books, 1989.

Have You Seen Any Good Miracles Lately? Phyllis Berman
Popkin. Available from author at R#1, Box 175-Y, Faber,
VA 22938.

The Psychic Sourcebook: How to Choose and Use a Psychic,
Frederick G. Levine. New York, NY; Warner Books, 1988.

Psychic Studies: A Christian's View, Michael Perry. San Bernardino, CA; Borgo Press, 1987.

Synchronicity: The Bridge Between Matter and Mind, F. David
Peat. New York, NY; Bantam Books, 1988.

The Unobstructed Universe, Stewart White. Available from
Ariel Press, 3854 Mason Road, Canal Winchester, OH 43110.

Venture Inward, Hugh Lynn Cayce. New York, NY; Harper &
Row, 1985.

BOOKS TO BROADEN YOUR UNDERSTANDING OF
PSYCHISM—CHILDREN

*The Secret Life of Kids: An Exploration into Their Psychic
Sense,* James W. Peterson. Wheaton, IL; Theosophical Publishing House, 1988.

Twelve, Elaine Kittredge (for children of all ages). Chicago, IL;
Optex, 1981.

Understanding and Developing Your Child's Natural Psychic

Abilities, Alex Tanous and Katherine Fair Donnelly. New York, NY; Fireside Books (Simon and Schuster), 1979.

A reputable psychic reader functions like a mirror, reflecting back to you what you put out and, like a flashlight, helping you to see your path more clearly. His or her job is to provide information and insight—nothing more. As in any other facet of life, don't believe everything you hear, and always seek another opinion. Here are some magazines and newsletters on the subject:

Atlantis Rising magazine, P.O. Box 441, Livingston, MT 59047.

Body, Mind and Spirit magazine, P.O. Box 701, Providence, RI 02901.

Fate magazine, P.O. Box 1940, 170 Future Way, Marion, OH 43305-1940.

The Insider newsletter, Parapsychological Services Institute, 5575B Chamblee Dunwoody Road, Suite 323, Atlanta, GA 30338; (404) 391-0991.

Intuition magazine, P.O. Box 460773, San Francisco, CA 94146.

Psi Today magazine, Foundation for Research on the Nature of Man, P.O. Box 6847, Durham, NC 27708; (919) 688-8241.

Woodrew Update newsletter, 448 Rabbit Skin Road, Waynesville, NC 28786. Greta Woodrew's books are *On a Slide of Light* (Macmillan Publishing Co., Inc., 1981) and *Memories of Tomorrow* (Dolphin Books, a division of Doubleday, 1988). Unusually practical material on psychism, survival issues, and extraterrestrials.

NEAR-DEATH EXPERIENCE

For more information about the near-death phenomenon, contact the **International Association For Near-Death Studies,**

Inc., P.O. Box 502, East Windsor Hill, CT 06028-0502; (860) 528-5144. The association has several brochures to offer, education and referral services, a journal, newsletter publications, plus a list of books written on the subject. They sponsor public interest and support groups throughout the U.S. and Europe. Their regional and national conferences are superb.

A book-and-audiotape dramatization for children on the subject is *The Door to the Secret City* by Kathleen J. Forti. Available from Kids Want Answers, Too!, 1544 Bay Point Drive, Virginia Beach, VA 23454.

REINCARNATION

SOME BOOKS FOR ADULTS

Beyond the Ashes: Cases of Reincarnation from the Holocaust, Rabbi Yonassan Gershom. Virginia Beach, VA; A.R.E. Press, 1992.

The Case for Reincarnation, Joe Fisher. New York, NY; Citadel Press, 1992.

Coming Back: A Psychiatrist Explores Past-Life Journeys, Raymond A. Moody, Jr. New York, NY; Bantam Books, 1992.

Eye of the Centaur, Barbara Hand Clow. St. Paul, MN; Llewellyn Publications, 1986.

Life Between Life, Joel L. Whitton, M.D., Ph.D., and Joe Fisher. New York, NY; Warner Books, 1986.

Many Lives, Many Masters, Brian Weiss, M.D. New York, NY; Simon and Schuster, 1988.

Past Life Regression Guidebook, Bettye Binder. Available from Reincarnation Books, P.O. Box 7781, Culver City, CA 90233.

The Search for Omm Sety: Reincarnation and Eternal Love, Jonathan Cott. Garden City, NY; Doubleday and Co., 1987.

SOME BOOKS FOR CHILDREN

The Fall of Freddie the Leaf, Leo Buscaglia, Ph.D. Thorofare, NJ; Charles G. Slack, Inc., 1982.

Grandfather Twilight, Barbara Berger. New York, NY; Putnam Publishing Group, 1986.

Hope for the Flowers, Trina Paulus. New York, NY; Paulist Press, 1972.

The Mountains of Tibet, Mordicai Gerstein. New York, NY; Harper's Junior Books, 1987.

SPECIALS

Association for Past Life Research and Therapies, Inc., P.O. Box 20151, Riverside, CA 92516-0151; (909) 784-1570.

Henry Leo Bolduc wrote *The Journey Within,* Virginia Beach, VA; Inner Traditions, 1988. He regularly offers workshops in Healing the Past/Building the Future, Self-Hypnosis, and The Inner Journey. Anything he does is of unusual quality and integrity. To get on his mailing list, write or call him at P.O. Box 88, Independence, VA 24348; (540) 655-4523.

SOUNDS AND LANGUAGE

Numerous research findings are now available concerning **how the spoken sound of language actually molds and shapes the human brain**. This fact is important and deserves more attention. It seems that most of the ancient languages were designed to elicit specific energetic responses in body and mind from each particular arrangement of tone, pitch, and vibration. Sanskrit, for instance, was designed to activate mass memory and spiritual recall through the stimulation of endocrine centers (chakras) and spinal energies (kundalini), plus the skeletal and nervous system. The real secret to its mystical power is the way

Sanskrit is pronounced. Hawaiian is the same way. Languages, like runes, which were unspoken, work through eye contact, touch, emotional response, and intuition to activate memory. Here are two very interesting books on the power of sound:

The Secret Power of Music, David Tame. New York, NY; Destiny Books, 1984.

Sound Health: The Music and Sounds That Make Us Whole, Steven Halpern with Louis Savary, San Francisco, CA; Harper & Row, 1985.

The **Institute For Music, Health & Education** is a place of miracles. Through experiential classroom involvement, students engage in accelerated learning and listening techniques that can and often do facilitate healing. "Music holds the rhythmic and tonal patterns of energy that directly organize thought, speech, and movement," says the institute's originator, Don G. Campbell. The author of seven books, including *Music and Miracles* and *Music: Physician for Times to Come,* Campbell is internationally known for his innovative techniques for helping people reclaim their health by changing their response to sound. To obtain a catalog of publications as well as workshop and class schedules, contact: Institute for Music, Health & Education, P.O. Box 1244, Boulder, CO 80306; (303) 443-8484.

SPIRITUALITY AND MEDITATION

Meditation is a helpful way to facilitate and maintain the inner journey based on commitment and discipline. It is not some brand name sold upon an open market of pie-in-the-sky promises. There is no quick high to be had and no one has a monopoly on the subject. Meditative life consists of phases and cycles as the process assists you with inner cleansing and inner purification. It changes as you change, yet meditation always offers the steadiness of spiritual growth. There are many techniques and countless styles. One of my favorite teachers is the practical and humorous **Eknath Easwaran**. His book *Meditation: Commonsense Directions for an Uncommon Life* is excellent. Founder of the Blue Mountain Center for Meditation and a popular college professor, Easwaran has written many books; they are available through Nilgiri Press, Box 256, Tomales, CA 94971; (707) 878-2749. Other Books on Meditation and Affirmative Prayer

Active Meditation, The Western Tradition, Robert R. Leichtman, M.D., and Carl Japikse. Canal Winchester, OH; Ariel Press, 1982.

An Easy Guide to Meditation, Roy Eugene Davis. Available from CSA Press, P.O. Box 7, Lake Rabun Road, Lakemont, GA 30552.

The Chakras, C.W. Leadbeater. Wheaton, IL; Knowledge Systems, Inc., 1988.

Chakras: Energy Centers of Transformation, Harish Johari. Rochester, VT; Destiny Books, 1987.

The Dynamic Laws of Prayer, Catherine Ponder. Available from DeVorss & Company, P.O. Box 550, Marina Del Rey, CA 90294.

Energy, Ecstasy, and Your Seven Vital Chakras, Bernard Gunther. North Hollywood, CA; Newcastle, 1983.

How to Meditate, Lawrence LeShan. New York, NY; Bantam Books, 1975.

The Miracle of Mindfulness: A Manual on Meditation, Thich Nhat Hanh. Boston, MA; Beacon Press, 1975.

My Magic Garden, Ilse Klipper (a meditation guide for children). Available from Science of Mind Publications, P.O. Box 75127, Los Angeles, CA 90075.

Receptive Prayer and *A Manual of Receptive Prayer,* both by Grace Adolphsen Brame. Available from Science of Mind Publications, P.O. Box 75127, Los Angeles, CA 90075.

Spirituality is based upon a personal, intimate experience of God. There are no standards or dogmas, only precedents, as individual knowing—or gnosis—is honored. Because it is so personal, methodologies are often elusive or confusing at best. So here is a caution to remember: **there is no system of spiritual enlightenment that can guarantee spiritual attainment.** Just because someone thinks he or she is spiritual doesn't mean that person is. Always look to the results, the consequences, for aftereffects cannot be faked. My own personal yardstick says, "If you can't live what you know to be true, then it isn't worth knowing."

The spiritual path is truly "The Inner Journey," deep within the depths of your inner self, and it entails a thorough "house cleaning" on every level of your being. The challenge is to find the God within and reconnect, and that means a lifetime commitment. Spirituality is a lifestyle, as well as a philosophic belief and inner knowing.

SOME BOOKS THAT ILLUMINATE THE SPIRITUAL PERSPECTIVE

As Above, So Below: Paths to Spiritual Renewal in Daily Life, by the editors of *New Age Journal.* Available from New Age Journal Book Order Dept., 342 Western Avenue, Brighton, MA 02135; (617) 787-2005.

Care of the Soul, Thomas Moore, New York, NY; HarperCollins, 1992.

The Coming of the Cosmic Christ, Matthew Fox. San Francisco, CA; Harper & Row, 1988.

A Course in Miracles, An unusual three-volume set now condensed into one and available commerically. New York, New York; Penguin Press, 1996. Interpretive materials available from Miracle Distribution Center, 1141 East Ash Avenue, Fullerton, CA 92631; (714) 738-8380.

Discovering Your Soul's Purpose, Mark Thurston. Available as a kit from A.R.E. Bookstore, P.O. Box 595, Virginia Beach, VA 23451; 1-800-723-1112. Also available from the same source is *Edgar Cayce's Story of the Soul,* W. H. Church.

Finding Your Life Mission: How to Unleash That Creative Power and Live with Intention, Naomi Stephan, Ph.D. Walpole, NH; Stillpoint Press, 1990.

Gently Lead: How to Teach Your Children About God While Finding Out for Yourself, Polly Berrien Berenda. New York, NY; HarperCollins, 1991.

Homesick for Heaven—You Don't Have to Wait! Walter Starcke. From Guadalupe Press, P.O. Box 865, Boerne, TX 78006.

Illusions, Richard Bach. New York, NY; Delacorte Press, 1977.

The Imprisoned Splendour, Raynor Johnson. Norwich, CT; Pelegrin Press (Pilgrim Books), 1989.

Kinship with All Life, J. Allen Boone. New York, NY; Harper & Row, 1976.

Mister God, This Is Anna, Fynn. New York, NY; Ballantine Books, 1974.

Ordinary People As Monks and Mystics: Lifestyles for Self-Discovery, Marsha Sinetar. Mahwah, NJ; Paulist Press, 1986.

Path with Heart: A Guide Through the Perils and Promises of Spiritual Life, Jack Kornfield. New York, NY; Bantam Books, 1993.

Practical Mysticism, Evelyn Underhill. Available from Ariel Press, 3854 Mason Road, Canal Winchester, OH 43110.

The Prophet, Kahlil Gibran. New York, NY; Alfred A. Knopf, continuous printings—a timeless classic!

The Re-enchantment of the World, Morris Berman. Ithaca, NY; Cornell University Press, 1981.

The Seat of the Soul, Gary Zukav. New York, NY; Simon and Schuster (A Fireside Book), 1990.

The Seeker's Handbook: The Complete Guide to Spiritual Pathfinding, John Lash. New York, NY; Harmony Books, 1990.

Talking with Nature, Michael J. Roads. Tiburon, CA; H.J. Kramer, Inc., 1987.

Walking a Sacred Path: Rediscovering the Labyrinth as a Spiritual Tool, Dr. Lauren Artress. New York, NY; Riverhead Books, 1995.

When You Can Walk on Water, Take the Boat, John Harricharan. Marietta, GA; New World Publishing, 1988.

Who Speaks for Wolf, Paula Underwood Spencer (for children of all ages). Available from Tribe of Two Press, P.O. Box 913, Georgetown, TX 78626. Any difficulty, call (415) 457-6548.

World Scripture: A Comparative Anthology of Sacred Texts, edited by Andrew Wilson. New York, NY; Paragon House, 1991.

VIDEOS

Mandalas, Vision of Heaven and Earth and *The Human Journey* feature the transformational sculpture of Mirtala set to music. From MACROmedia, P.O. Box 279, Epping, NH 03042. To obtain a copy of Mirtala's brochure, write: Mirtala, P.O. Box 3237, Sedona, AZ 86336-3237.

Nicholas Roerich: Messenger of Beauty features the visionary paintings of Nicholas Roerich set to music. Of unusual quality. From Nicholas Roerich Museum, 319 West 107th Street, New York, NY 10025-2799; (212) 864-7752.

STORYTELLING

Storytelling is an ancient skill. Through its use, great truths and wisdoms were once conveyed, along with proper codes of conduct and morals. I am happy to say that this wonderful art form and teaching tool is undergoing a comeback. For more information, contact: National Storytelling Association, P.O. Box 309, Jonesborough, TN 37659; (615) 753-2171 or 1-800-525-4514.

SOME BOOKS ON STORYTELLING

Awakening the Hidden Storyteller: How to Build a Storytelling Tradition in Your Family, Robin Moore. Boston, MA; Shambhala, 1991.

Sacred Stories: A Celebration of the Power of Stories to Transform and Heal, edited by Anne Simpkinson and Charles Simpkinson. San Francisco, CA; Harper/San Francisco, 1993.

Spinning Tales, Weaving Hope: Stories of Peace, Justice and the Environment, edited by Ed Brody, Jay Goldspinner, Katie Green, Rona Leventhal, and John Porcino. Available from New Society Publishers, 4527 Springfield Avenue, Philadelphia, PA 19143.

Storytelling & the Art of Imagination, Nancy Mellon. London, England; Element Books, 1992 (also available in the U.S.).

What the Bee Knows: Reflections on Myth, Symbol and Story, P.L. Travers. New York, NY; Penguin Books, 1993.

Wisdom of the Heart, an audiotape of storytelling by Carol McCormick and available through Dancing Spirit Studio, 625 Windemere Drive, Plymouth, MN 55441; (612) 546-4133.

NATIVE AMERICAN STORIES AS ORAL HISTORY

Paula Underwood is the oral historian for her family's Native American tradition. She has inherited the responsibility for this oral history, which comes to her from her grandfather's grandmother, who committed it to memory in the early 1800s and meticulously handed it down through five generations. Tested since childhood by her father, to make certain she could restate this oral history in contemporary language so the children's children could understand, she was finally led to commit this precious heritage to paper. The result is *The Walking People, A Native American Oral History,* covering ten thousand years of migration—literally a journey of epic proportions. I consider this book to be of monumental importance! To obtain a copy, contact: A Tribe of Two Press, P.O. Box 913, Georgetown, TX 78627. Should you have any difficulty ordering, call (415) 457-6548 in San Anselmo, California for assistance. They also handle her children's book, *Who Speaks for Wolf.*

THE OLD WAYS

The word "pagan" simply means "country dweller" in Latin and refers to a more natural, harmonious way of living in accord with the rhythm of life as we know it on the earthplane. This particular viewpoint honors natural systems and cycles, the kingdoms of our little brothers and sisters (minerals, plants, animals), and the spirit keepers. It emphasizes intuition and sacredness and ritual. Here are some good references along this line of thinking:

Drawing Down the Moon, Margot Adler. New York, NY; Viking Press, 1979.

Dreaming the Dark, Starhawk. Boston, MA; Beacon Press, 1982.

Dreamwalker, Mary Summer Rain. Norfolk, VA; Donning Co., 1988.

Phoenix Rising: No-Eyes' Vision of the Changes to Come, Mary Summer Rain. Norfolk, VA; Donning Co., 1987.

The Spiral Dance: A Rebirth of the Ancient Religion of the Great Goddess, Starhawk. New York, NY; Harper & Row, 1979.

Spirit Song: The Visionary Wisdom of No-Eyes, Mary Summer Rain. Norfolk, VA; Donning Co., 1985.

The Way of the Shaman, Michael Harner. New York, NY; Bantam Books, 1982.

OTHER SOURCES FOR LEARNING ABOUT "THE OLD WAYS"

Circle Network News, P.O. Box 219, Mt. Horeb, WI 53572; (608) 924-2216.

Dance of the Deer Foundation, Center for Shamanic Studies, P.O. Box 699, Soquel, CA 95073; (408) 475-9560.

Enchanté magazine, 30 Charlton Street, Box 6F, New York, NY 10014.

Foundation for Shamanic Studies, The, Box 670, Norwalk, CT 06852; (203) 454-2825.

The Free Spirit Alliance, P.O. Box 5358, Laurel, MD 20726-5358; (301) 604-6049.

Magical Blend magazine, P.O. Box 600, Chico, CA 95927; (916) 893-9037.

Page Bryant, Earth Studies and The Star Shields, 707 Brunswick Drive, Waynesville, NC 28786.

Shaman's Drum magazine, P.O. Box 430, Willits, CA 95490; For subscriptions, phone (707) 459-0486.

Twylah Nitsch (Grandmother of the Wolf Clan of the Seneca Nation), 12199 Brant-Reservation Road, Irving, NY 14081; (716) 549-3889.

Wildfire magazine, P.O. Box 8584, Seminole, FL 34645; (813) 581-5911.

THE WORK OF P.M.H. ATWATER, Lʜ.D.

Coming Back to Life: The Aftereffects of the Near-Death Experience, Dodd, Mead & Company, 1988 (hardcover); Ballantine Books, 1989 (paperback).

The Magical Language of Runes, Bear & Company, 1990 (softcover).

Beyond the Light, The Mysteries and Revelations of the Near-Death Experience, Birch Lane Press, 1994 (hardcover); Avon Books, 1995 (paperback).

Future Memory: How Those Who "See the Future" Shed New Light on the Workings of the Human Mind. Birch Lane Press, 1996 (hardcover).

The Aftereffects of the Near-Death Experience, a talk about the positive and negative aftereffects of the near-death phenomenon, given to a live audience. From YOU CAN Change Your Life, P.O. Box 7691, Charlottesville, VA 22906-7691.

Audiotapes: *Coming Back to Life* updates her first book. *As You Die* talks an individual through the stages of physical death and the separation of the soul. Both audiotapes are available from Mithra Corporation, P.O. Box 447, Organ, NM 88052-0447.

YOU CAN Change Your Life, P.O. Box 7691, Charlottesville, VA 22906-7691. This is Atwater's business address. To sponsor one of her talks or workshops, and to receive a brochure about her services, send a stamped, self-addressed #10 envelope to the above address. (Her audio and video tapes are also available from her, as well as from Mithra.)

P.M.H. Atwater specializes in rune castings by telephone

from her home. Or, you can reach her on the nation's largest psychic 900-line, "Psychic Friends Network." Just dial 1-900-737-3225. The present charge is $3.89 per minute with a twenty-minute limit per call. Her on-duty hours are updated regularly.

Runegiver

Dana Corby, 1774 Rainier Avenue South, Suite 30, Seattle, WA 98144. The one who passed rune use on to me is now offering a new way of creating rune sets—with art glass, and in an astounding range of colors. Included in each set she fashions is her booklet entitled *The Witches' Runes*. You can contact her directly for more information, if you desire.

I never had the privilege of taking a class from Dana Corby; all I was able to do was view her castings from a distance. The set she prepared for me had but a small sheet enclosed with keyword meanings for each glyph, and that's all. My interpretations of the glyphs are based on my research, on inner promptings when the runes "spoke" to me, and on what I observed with others during castings and playshops. Whatever I have done with this ancient system, I have done in love. And to Dana Corby I say "Thank you!" What you once gave to me, I can now give to others.

Runecutters

Carole Anderson, P.O. Box 27, Hill, NH 03243. Should you wish to have a runestone set created "the elder way," Carole Anderson specializes in this. Through ritual and meditation, she is prompted to place the proper glyph to the right stone. She uses only river pebbles similar to those I have. Contact her directly.

Leslie Anne Dressler, c/o YOU CAN Change Your Life, P.O. Box 7691, Charlottesville, VA 22906-7691. Leslie Anne Dressler is a professional historian who makes artifact reproductions of stunning quality. She works intuitively in stone and with many other mediums. Your choice. Contact her directly.

Don Joseph, Pendragons, A Moment in Time, 310 Wells Ave. South, Renton, WA 98055; (206) 271-9909. As creator of the runestones used in Kevin Costner's movie *Robin Hood*, Don Joseph has also devised several styles of Goddess Runes. Contact him directly. His store, *Pendragons, A Moment in Time,* is worth noting as he created a castle complete with moat on the inside, emphasizing the magic of Avalon. Stop by if you're in the area, for the store is truly unique.

Notes

1. Cro-Magnon people: a summary of new findings in *Newsweek* magazine, November 10, 1986, cover feature entitled "The Way We Were," pages 62–72. To contact *Newsweek,* write or call them at 251 West 57th Street, New York, NY 10019; (212) 445-4120. Also refer to the intriguing book *The Man in the Ice, The Amazing Inside Story of the 5,000-Year-Old Body Found Trapped in a Glacier in the Alps,* Konrad Spindler (leader of the scientific investigation that found the body). London, England; Weidenfeld and Nicolson, 1994.
2. *Allmutter,* Herman Wirth. No translation from German available, by request of his estate. Wirth was pro-Nazi during World War II. Hitler used this research to back up his claim of Aryan race superiority and had rune signs painted or carved onto equipment and property he deemed important. Many of the Gestapo were taught the rune spells of Futhark for the purpose of infusing the Third Reich with supernatural powers. During the war, runes were synonymous with Naziism. The downfall of Hitler freed the ancient glyphs from this perversion, but it wasn't until the publication of Ralph Blum's *The Book of Runes* in 1982 that rune was redeemed.
3. *The Language of the Goddess,* Marija Gimbutas. San Francisco, CA; Harper & Row, 1989.

4. *The Civilization of the Goddess: The World of Old Europe,* Marija Gimbutas. San Francisco, CA; Harper/San Francisco, 1991. Note the chapter on "The Sacred Script," and especially pages 314 and 320–321.

5. *The Key,* John Philip Cohane. New York, NY; Crown, 1969.

6. *The Celts,* Gerhard Herm. New York, NY; St. Martin's Press, 1975. Note pages 72–74, where he discusses the Ur-people.

7. Winfred P. Lehmann quotes from an article written by *The New York Times* newspaper columnist William Safire, dated November 29, 1987, and entitled "Scholars Attempt to Discover Roots of Language Spoken 50,000 Years Ago."

8. *The Once and Future Star,* George Michanowsky. New York, NY; Hawthorn Books, 1977.

9. *Before Columbus: Links Between the Old World & Ancient America,* Cyrus Herzl Gordon. New York, NY; Crown, 1971. To continue this thought about the almost encyclopedic meanings of early alphabet characters, refer to Revelations 13:17–18 in the Christian Bible, where it is revealed that the number 666 is the code name for "the beast." In Aramaic, the language of the Bible, every alphabet letter also stood for a number. By employing the numerical system used then, we determine that the number 666 literally spells out a man's name, and that name is NRON KSR, a spelling popular at that time for—Nero Caesar.

10. This quote is from *Man, Myth & Magic: An Illustrated Encyclopedia of the Supernatural,* edited by Richard Cavendish (Volume 1, section on "Alphabets," pages 69–72). New York, NY; Marshall-Cavendish Corporation, 1970.

11. *Secret of the Runes,* translated and edited by Stephen E. Flowers (from the 1908 classic by renowned historian and Indo-European linguist Guido von List). Rochester, VT; Destiny Books, 1988.
    Runes, Ralph W.V. Elliot. New York, NY; Philosophical Library, 1959.
    The Vikings and Their Origins, David M. Wilson. New

York, NY; McGraw-Hill Book Co., 1970.

Futhark: A Handbook of Rune Magic, Edred Thorsson. York Beach, ME; Weiser Books, 1984.

Runelore: A Handbook of Esoteric Runology, Edred Thorsson. York Beach, ME; Weiser Books, 1986.

At the Well of Wyrd: A Handbook of Runic Divination, Edred Thorsson. York Beach, ME; Weiser Books, 1988.

12. *America B.C.,* Barry Fell. New York, NY; Pocket Books, 1976.

Before Civilization, Colin Renfrew. New York, NY; Alfred A. Knopf, 1974.

The New View Over Atlantis, John Michel. New York, NY; Harper & Row, 1983.

Ogam, the Poets' Secret, Sean O'Boyle. Published by Gilbert Dalton and available from The Dowser's Bookstore, P.O. Box 4, Danville, VT 05828-0024; (802) 684-1176.

Ogam, Consaine & Tifinag Alphabets—Ancient Uses, Warren W. Dexter. Rutland, VT; Academy Books, 1984.

The Runes and Other Magical Alphabets, Michael E. Howard. London, England; Aquarian Press, 1978 (handled in the U.S. by Sterling Publishers, New York).

13. *Missing Links Discovered in Assyrian Tablets* and *King Solomon's Temple,* both books by E. Raymond Capt, and available through Artisan Sales, P.O. Box 1497, Thousand Oaks, CA 91358-0497; (805) 491-0936.

14. Frank C. Tribbe's article entitled "Was Glastonbury a Stepping Stone?" appeared in *Glastonbury Treasures,* edited by Donald L. Cyr, and available from Stonehenge Viewpoint, 800 Palermo Drive, Santa Barbara, CA 93105. My thanks to Tribbe for his kindness in pointing out to me this additional link with the runes I use.

15. This quote appears on page 166 of *Everyday Life in the Viking Age,* Jacqueline Simpson. New York, NY; G.P. Putnam's Sons, 1967.

16. For Mayan Connections to Odin/Wotan legends, search out *Sacred Mysteries Among the Mayans and the Quiches*

11,500 Years Ago, Augustus Le Plongeon. New York, NY; Robert Macoy, 1886.

17. There are five of these books by J.R.R. Tolkien. *The Hobbit, or There and Back Again.* Boston, MA; Houghton Mifflin Company, 1984. *The Lord of the Rings* (a three-volume set). Boston, MA; Houghton Mifflin Company, 1965. Finally, *The Silmarillion.* Boston, MA; Houghton Mifflin Company, 1977.

18. *Just So Stories,* Rudyard Kipling. New York, NY; Weathervane Books, 1978.

19. *The Book of Runes,* Ralph Blum (includes ceramic glyphs and pouch). New York, NY; St. Martin's Press, 1987. And *The New Book of Runes,* Ralph Blum. New York, NY; St. Martin's Press, 1987. A recent update is *The Healing Runes: Tools for the Recovery of Body, Mind, Heart & Soul,* Ralph H. Blum and Susan Loughan. New York, NY; St. Martin's Press, 1995.

20. *The Magical Language of Runes,* P.M.H. Atwater. Originally self-published, numerous printings. Picked up as a softcover edition by Bear & Company, Santa Fe, NM, 1990; now out of print.

21. I was one of the original psychic counselors when the Professional Psychic Counselors Network (Psychic Friends) came on-line. They featured me in their first two infomercials that were aired nationally for a year and a half. (Yes, I was that "light-haired" grandmother type sitting on the floor tossing rocks—rune casting.) I don't know how other psychic counselors operate their business on the line, but I endeavor to be of service in helping people gain more clarity in their decision-making process and to offer inspiration when needed. I have never conducted myself as some fortune-teller trying to amaze anyone. For those who want such entertainment, I simply request that they hang up, re-dial, and seek out someone else more suited to that type of performance. If a practical psychic with a hearty laugh and a gentle voice interests you, call me sometime. Dial 1-900-737-3225, then punch in extension 7039. There is a re-

cording to tell you when I am next on duty. At this writing, there is a charge of $3.89 *per minute* that you will be billed for the call, and it will appear on your monthly telephone statement.

22. The E. Otha Wingo quote was carried in the Autumn 1984 issue of *Huna Work International.* Huna Research, Inc. (founded in 1945 by Max Freedom Long) is headquartered at 1760 Anna Street, Cape Girardeau, MO 63701; (573) 334-3478.

23. A good definition of "anomalies" can be found in *Mysteries of the Explained,* published by Reader's Digest in 1982: "Any departure from the expected arrangement, general rule, or usual method is considered to be an anomaly." The International Fortean Organization specializes in anomalies. Although membership-oriented, they welcome inquiries and information searches. Contact them through INFO, P.O. Box 367, Arlington, VA 22210-0367. The best book of more recent vintage on the subject is *Forbidden Archaeology,* Michael A. Cremo and Richard L. Thompson. Badger, CA; Govardhan Hill, 1993.

24. *The Letters of J.R.R. Tolkien,* selected and edited by Humphrey Carpenter with the assistance of Christopher Tolkien. Boston, MA; Houghton Mifflin Company, 1981.

25. *A New Science of Life: The Hypothesis of Formative Causation,* Rupert Sheldrake. Los Angeles, CA; J.P. Tarcher/ Houghton Mifflin, 1981. Also important to consider is the new science of chaos. Refer to *Chaos: Making a New Science,* James Gleick. New York, NY; Viking Press, 1987. And *A Turbulent Mirror: An Illustrated Guide to the Chaos Theory & the Science of Wholeness,* John Briggs and F. David Peat. New York, NY; Harper & Row, 1989.

26. This quote from Simon Henderson's article "Simon's Spiral" was featured in the Fall 1987 edition of *Wildfire* magazine. *Wildfire* used to be produced by The Bear Tribe (P.O. Box 9167, Spokane, WA 99209), but exists today as a separate publication. Write: *Wildfire,* P.O. Box 8584, Seminole, FL 34645. Feel free to contact them for back issues.

27. Jean Auel's Earth Children Series was published by Crown in New York City. Her books are *The Clan of the Cave Bear* (1980), *The Valley of Horses* (1982), *The Mammoth Hunters* (1985), and *The Plains of Passage* (1990).

28. *Runes of the North,* Sigurd F. Olson. New York, NY; Alfred A. Knopf, 1985. Should you have any trouble finding this book, it is now available through Random House; call 1-800-733-3000.

29. *Illuminations of Hildegard of Bingen* (Matthew Fox); *Hildegard of Bingen's Medicine* (Strehlow); *Hildegard of Bingen's Book of Divine Works* and *Hildegard of Bingen's Scivias* (Know the Ways); *Meditations with Hildegard of Bingen* (Gabriele Uhlein)—all published by Bear & Company, P.O. Drawer 2860, Santa Fe, NM 87504-2860.

30. *Women Who Run With the Wolves: Myths and Stories of the Wild Woman Archetype,* Clarissa Pinkola Estés, Ph.D. New York, NY; Ballantine Books, 1992.

31. *New Age Journal* magazine, 42 Pleasant Street, Watertown, MA 02172; (617) 926-0200.

32. *Stories from the Motherline: Reclaiming the Mother-Daughter Bond, Finding Our Feminine Souls,* Naomi Ruth Lowinsky, Ph.D. (renamed *The Motherline: Everywoman's Journey to Find Her Female Roots,* in the softcover edition). Los Angeles, CA; J.P. Tarcher, 1992.

33. *Hymns to an Unknown God: Awakening the Spirit in Everyday Life,* Sam Keen. New York, NY; Bantam Books, 1994.

man/male

woman/female

love/harmony

marriage/union

home/tradition

confusion

conflict

money/ego

comfort/safety

fire/passion

gifts/talents

beneficial gain

female questioner

male questioner

negativity

change

GODDESS RUNES

Affix these labels to flat stones or other objects appropriate for casting to create your own rune set. Trim excess paper around runes to size of object. Cutouts are not meant to convey size or shape of object used.